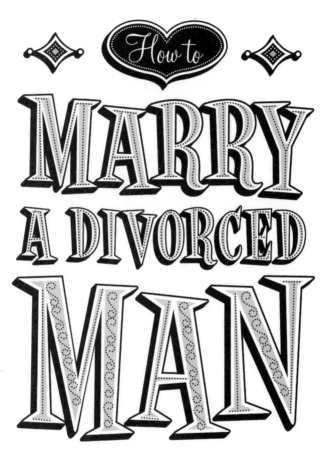

How to

MARRY A DIVORCED MAN

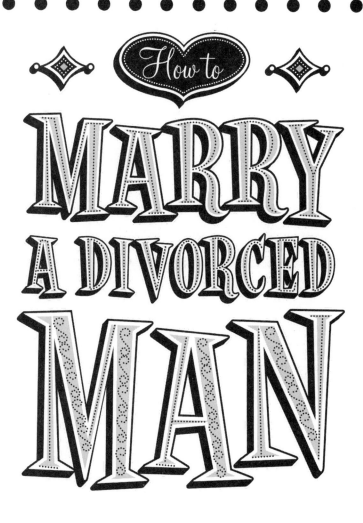

How to MARRY A DIVORCED MAN

LESLIE FRAM

ReganBooks
An Imprint of HarperCollins*Publishers*

HarperCollins books may be purchased for educational, business, or sales promotional use. For information please write: Special Markets Department, HarperCollins Publishers Inc., 10 East 53rd Street, New York, NY 10022.

FIRST EDITION

Printed on acid-free paper

Library of Congress Cataloging-in-Publication Data

Fram, Leslie.
How to marry a divorced man / Leslie Fram.—1st ed.
p. cm.
ISBN 0-06-009032-4
1. Mate selection.   2. Divorced men.
3. Remarriage.   I. Title.

HQ801 .F673   2002
646.7'7—dc21
2002031804

03 04 05 06 07 WBC/RRD 10 9 8 7 6 5 4 3 2 1

To *my* Divorced Man, the love of my life,
my husband, who is in no way responsible for
any of this material, but whose loving
encouragement enabled me to get it all down
anyway. And to darling baby, Stanford, whose
sunshine face is the prize at the end of the journey.

Contents

PART I

WHY I WROTE THIS BOOK

1. A Personal Tale

This book was born from my very own saga. It has been a journey of transformation, from being single, to finding "the one," to marrying, to almost murdering, to almost divorcing, to learning to cope, to discovering a sense of empowerment, to finally being able to find fulfillment in loving a Divorced Man.

Before I knew it, I was in my mid-thirties. All my adult life, I worked diligently to accomplish my educational, career, and financial goals. I got an M.B.A.; I was a senior executive at a media company; and I purchased an apartment in New York City. Yes, things had finally fallen into place. At this stage of my life, I could honestly say that I was happy with myself. Even my mother and I finally agreed on something—it was time for me to find a husband. I approached this mission in the same way I approached all my other personal successes: with a clear goal, a strategy, and a lot of passion.

The search was on. My initial survey of the available male landscape—primarily formulated by going on lots of lousy dates and commiserating with other disgruntled single girlfriends—concluded that at my age, two main groups prevailed: perpetual bachelors and divorcés. At first, I beelined into the arms of thirty-five-plus-year-old bachelors, hoping that I would be the woman special enough to save them from their loner ways. What was I thinking?! As much as they tell you that they "want to settle down with the right woman," they actually would rather be pouncing on one unsuspecting female, then another. Years later, those very same bachelors are still toxically single. Take my advice and stay away.

Alas, given the paltry selection of marriage material out there, Divorced Men seemed to be the only viable prospects. I opened myself up to the inevitable. Then, as if right on cue, I promptly proceeded to fall in love with one. He was loving, intelligent, fun, and ready for commitment. After almost one year of courtship, we were ecstatically engaged. I was right on track in achieving my objective. Hey, Mom, I might get married after all!

Then I experienced a rude awakening and my plan nearly fell apart. When I read his divorce agreement, I almost called the wedding off. *"You pay your X how much f***ing money per month?"* My fiancé's seemingly ample income was more than halved by these payments and I quickly understood that our future together would similarly suffer. Meanwhile, his X had never worked a day in her adult life. It also seemed ludicrous that his ten-year-old son had an annual income from child-support payments that was higher than mine. To make matters worse, I noticed that the more intimate my man and I became, the more he felt the need to visit his X and kids in his old house—even when they were not there. Did he miss his old cat, his room, his bed, his X? And why was she telephoning him with increasing frequency? More important, why was he taking her calls? What was going on?!

My angst propelled me to look for assistance in bookstores, but I found none. I felt too ashamed to discuss these financial inequities and my husband-to-be's bizarre behavior with anyone other than New York City cabbies. After all, I was supposed to be a blushing bride preparing for the most special day of my entire life. Who was I to complain? I soon realized that this was only the beginning and I was not sure I could handle what lay beyond. So much for plotting ahead.

Upon carefully weighing the pros and cons, I did decide to wed my Divorced Man after all. I determined that despite the monetary mess and emotional madness that came with his divorced life, he was the soulmate I had been searching for and I couldn't let him go. These first four married years have been the most blissful, yet frequently challenging—okay, I will not lie to you, *hellish*—I have ever had. The truth is that after we exchanged our nuptial vows, his irrational actions resulting from his divorce intensified. I felt like the loneliest newlywed who was ever carried across a threshold—but my *threshold* was not the one transitioning me into the proverbial marital home, it was a threshold of rage.

I kept asking myself, "Is this what I waited for?" I couldn't help but feel stupid for making such an unenlightened, yet all-important, decision. On countless occasions, I was thrown into deep bouts of Oreo-gorging despair, pitying myself for loving a man with so much baggage. I thought that if only I could be more understanding, love him more, cater to him more, then his postdivorce trauma would disappear—what a worthless idea! So many times I wanted to strangle him when I felt his psychoconstipation from his earlier marriage rudely invade our present, and future, together. Sometimes, I even dreamed of how life could be sweeter if I just became a casualty of divorce myself. Others might call surviving his divorce-related afflictions *rewarding* or *character building,* but I ask you, who wanted to be rewarded with so much character? Not I, thank you very much.

After a tumultuous four years of marriage to my Divorced Man, our love is stronger than ever. It has been, and often continues to be, a painful voyage, but with our solid commitment to each other we now know how to work through his divorce-related issues. *Whew!* I never imagined I could ever say that. Against the disquieting odds that over 60 percent of second marriages fail due to the unresolved issues the remarried partner brings into the second marriage, we have survived. We are each other's one and only.

Had I been primed as to what to expect from my Divorced Man, had I known how to handle his divorce legacies more intelligently, I would have better managed my relationship from the start. Only then could I have guaranteed our love without enduring many precious years of emotional strain. If only I had known what you are about to know, Dear Reader, I would have been much better off and saved thousands of dollars in shrink bills. But then again, had I not gone through the journey with him, I could not have written *How to Marry a Divorced Man* and *you* would not have benefited from the wisdom in this book.

◆ 2. Women on the Verge ◆

Women involved with Divorced Men will soon represent a majority of the adult female population. Show some respect!

It turns out that I am not alone. National statistics show that there is a growing trend of women postponing their first marriage in order to pursue their educational, financial, and career dreams. Plus, with half of all marriages ending in divorce, there is a great probability that each of the seventy million women in the United States between the ages of eighteen and fifty-four will date or marry a Divorced Man sometime during her lifetime. In fact, more than 40 percent of U.S. marriages involve one spouse who has been married at least once before. Combine this data and you have the genesis of a demographic comprised of women like myself who, when finally ready to marry for the first time, are marrying Divorced Men, men who are already on their second time around. We may be older, wiser, and more self-sufficient than women have ever been, but our prized independence also makes us less tolerant and even ill-equipped to deal with the numerous emotional, time, and money constraints, not to mention the downright outrage, that comes with dating and marrying a Divorced Man. In other words, we may know how to finesse a last-minute upgrade from coach to first class with a window seat, but when we enter a relationship with a Divorced Man, we are totally clueless.

Historically, women involved with Divorced Men have played second fiddle to the first wife, who is most often the biological mother of his children. Does being the first partner for his practice run at matrimony make her a superior person to you? I think not. And yet, consistently, the media and our society at large have portrayed us as Machiavellian home wreckers. Recall Cinderella's evil stepmother, a stereotype we were all exposed to as children—a tale no doubt fueled by first-wife propagandists. God forbid your income is not as high as your Divorced Man's, or you are just a day younger or a tad prettier than his first wife. The derogatory labels abound: bimbo, trophy wife, gold digger; I've even heard the word *stepmonster* bandied about. Now consider the reality: Only an emotionally giving and mature person could possibly put up with all the miseries attached to loving a man while inheriting his X and his children.

As a result of this undeserving subordination, the protocol has been for millions of women to grin and bear the emotional challenges related to their Divorced Men. From childhood on, we have all been taught that it is unladylike to complain, or to initiate, or perpetuate conflict. Instead, we were told that our role was to please and *make nice* so that we would be liked by our classmates, teachers, suitors, coworkers, bosses, and, sooner or later, husbands.

But between playing in the schoolyard and entering married life, you find you have had little recourse in dealing with the dilemmas surrounding the Divorced Man in your life. You can't talk to your mom about it, she's just thrilled that you are en route to getting married and will tell you to do whatever it takes to maintain that status. Your single girlfriends tell you to quit ranting because, "You should be thankful that at least you have a steady man in your life." And your married girlfriends, especially those with children, can't be bothered by your naiveté in such matters; besides, their hands are full with enough emotional freight of their own.

Unanimously, the women I queried for *HTMADM* woefully acknowledged that there was zero to little guidance during their times of need. Like myself, they were forced to improvise all alone through their Divorced Men's tribulations—often with disastrous results. Without consulting others who have lived through similar situations, what woman would know how to adroitly handle a stalking X? Or the daughter of your Divorced Man who feels entitled, without your permission, to walk out of the house wearing your favorite dress? Or a lover who takes a phone call from his X during coitus?

And yet, suffering in silence is antithetical to women's natural inclination to commune with others. Once women involved with Divorced Men find a willing outlet—watch out! Try casually mentioning that your husband has an X to a virtual stranger and if hers has one too, it's as if you've uttered the secret password. She will immediately open up and spew forth, like a long dormant geyser that has spontaneously erupted, her most private X-tales of woe. All of us are in need of a good ol' cathartic bitch session every now and then. It is a strong bonding occasion. In fact, I have met several of my new best friends this way.

I don't know about you, but I am sick and tired of hearing the misnomers *second* wives and *step*mothers. In fact, there is no longer anything *step* about us. For the first time in history, we now represent a critical mass. According to the latest U.S. census, there are three times more families with second marriages than there are "traditional families." Ever growing in numbers, we can proactively change the prevailing antiquated perception by instituting a new and positive public image for ourselves. *Step*women? *Step*mothers? *Second* wives? That sounds dreadful. Let us now banish these deprecating *second* and *step* references from our vocabulary. A bona fide movement such as ours warrants a new name, so why not rename ourselves with a title that befits our affirmative and notable stance— how about *FateMates?* Yes, it has a nice ring to it. I'll go ahead and use this appellation for the rest of the book and centuries to come.

With the knowledge that we are strong, loving, capable, and deserving, let us no longer tiptoe through our men's divorce-legacy difficulties. The seventies ushered in women's lib, the eighties heard the cry from battered wives, in the nineties it was female victims of sexual harrassment, and now, in the twenty-first century, with the publication of *HTMADM*, FateMates will finally feel legitimized and will discover our public voice. Together, we represent a united front that shall be finally recognized and esteemed, as is our due. Hear us *roar!*

◆ 3. Mission Control ◆

Meet, mate, and be married.

No matter what phase your relationship is in, *HTMADM* enables you to enrich your prospects for marriage with your Divorced Man. You will be able to anticipate and know exactly how to champion all situations related to him. Whether you are contemplating targeting Divorced Men because of their high propensity for remarriage, or have had a few dates with a Divorced Man and are wondering what the future might entail, or are already in love with a Divorced Man and yearn to hear those wedding bells chime, or, even, are already married to a Divorced Man and need to steer him back on track—this book is for you.

This guidebook is the objective filter you need to make sense of all the anxiety-producing experiences and conflicting emotions you will brave for the love of your Divorced Man. So, rather than become a victim of his internal chaos, with the knowledge, tools, and confidence you acquire from *HTMADM, you* become the captain of your destiny together.

Here's how you'll benefit from *HTMADM:*

GAIN THE UPPER HAND
In order to master a Divorced Man, you need to be that much smarter. You'll have to discern his special qualities and handle him

accordingly so that you are the one seizing control of the relationship. Once you do, you're golden. *HTMADM* provides you with the know-how and techniques to accomplish this. The book breaks down the FateMate plight into basic elements, rendering it as unemotional as possible so that you can deal with his irrational reactions to situations simply and logically. You will find that his seemingly odd behavior will become transparent to you as his inner life sheds its mystery.

GET STRATEGIC

HTMADM asks: Why can't women *also* be calculating? Throughout history, men have always been expert at manipulating women during the dating game. To satisfy their less than cerebral instincts, men prey upon women's dreams for everlasting love. From puberty on, they figure out exactly what to say and do, whatever it takes to land us where they want us—usually in their beds. They know how to push our buttons to get us to swoon and succumb, particularly early in the dating cycle when our hopes run high. And yet, against all sanity tests and other empirical evidence, why do we continue to flat out melt with dreams of an idyllic future together every time a man softly whispers in our ears one of the following: "I would like to take you to visit: a) my mother; b) my kids; c) my weekend house in the Hamptons; d) the new three-bedroom apartment I am considering purchasing; or e) my tailor"?

It is comforting to know that after years of being secluded in a marriage, Divorced Men typically forget how to work at dating. They've been through a lot and are no longer savvy about the single men's scheming ways. In other words, he's yours for the taking. So, instead of being vulnerable to men's calculating tactics, this book teaches you how to reverse this by empowering you to rein him in and steer him toward becoming the man you've always dreamed of. FateMates, take advantage of it while you can.

Divorced Men are trembling at the thought of *HTMADM*'s publication. And personally, I love the sound of men's chattering teeth, don't you?

Win His Love and Respect

You cannot possibly rely on him to walk you through what he's feeling, since, as you will learn in Chapter 6, he is entirely oblivious and in abject denial of the emotional ramifications generated by his divorce. Unbeknownst to your Divorced Man in his repressed state, you will subtly navigate the course of your romance to where you want it as you simultaneously liberate him from his past. Ultimately, he will marvel at how well you understand him, be inspired by your astute insight, respect your intelligence for being able to release him from his prior life, and, finally, be free to love you as you want him to.

Gauge If He's the One

Ah, but does he deserve you? Do you really want him? You may or may not have him wrapped around your soon-to-be-engaged finger, but it's time to step back and objectively reassess whether he's worth any further investment. You discover that between his X and his kids, as well as his time and money constraints, he needs Arnold Schwarzenegger to carry his cargo. With his continuing commitments from his first marriage, can he give you enough of what you need to be fulfilled? Are there more pros than cons in this relationship? Is he recycled goods or a keeper? Are the trade-offs worth it to you? By the way, do you truly know what you require in a relationship to make you happy? The choice is yours.

MAXIMIZE YOUR LEVERAGE

The sooner you implement the teaching from *HTMADM,* the farther you will be able to advance your relationship with your Divorced Man. Even if you are in the lovey-dovey stages of your romance and believe nothing could possibly go wrong, do not pass Go until you heed the advice in this book. It may not be apparent at this juncture in your relationship, but if you do not follow the guidelines outlined in this book *now*—and it's never too late to start applying *HTMADM*'s winning tactics—you put your love with your Divorced Man at risk. Here's why: In the throes of courtship and lust, he's more willing to change, grow, and learn—*anything* to get the girl—especially before you have sex. This is when you have the leverage and this is when you should milk it for all it's worth. After commitment, men don't think they have to work as hard. Their personal strides become more difficult and infrequent as they grow habituated to comfortable patterns within the relationship. Subconsciously their logic tells them, "She already committed to me, therefore she loves me as I am, so I don't need to change." At this point, FateMate, you've already lost the majority of your pull in the relationship and you are at a disadvantage.

TAKE PREVENTIVE MEASURES

As you get deeper into the relationship, you become more intimate and therefore more vulnerable. And so does he. But when he feels emotionally unprotected, he is then apt to subliminally perceive your FateMate relationship as a major threat to his universe, i.e., the one he has been accustomed to that features his past married life with his X and his children. For him, the past is safer because it's familiar. Remember, you are still a relatively unknown entity to him. Like most men when they feel threatened, whether divorced or never married, he will instinctively pull away from anything new, i.e., you. Instead of pioneering and going forward, he will fervently cling to this former world—even though it no longer exists—except in his mind. This reaction, despite being wholly dysfunctional and self-sabotaging, as it inhibits him from moving toward a happy future with a FateMate, is, sadly, common.

He starts calling his X every day on your vacation together in Italy and talks of cutting the trip short because he feels guilty about missing his son's football game back home. Go ahead and laugh, but I could not have made this up! It's bewildering and downright infuriating. If you do not understand where he is coming from, you are apt to go berserk and jump on the next plane home. Or, better yet, drive him to the airport and stay behind living la dolce vita with that handsome gondolier. And who could blame you? Otherwise, much arguing would ensue, your mutual trust would be jeopardized, the anger would escalate, and you would eventually become estranged from your lover, which you could never have foreseen. All this could have been avoided with earlier assistance from *HTMADM*.

Attempts to restore a love gone sour are always more precarious than proper handling *before* or *at* the time the conflict occurs. Couples typically enlist the aid of self-help books and therapists at the eleventh hour, when too much lost time has elapsed, too much pain has been endured, and it's too late to salvage the love. *HTMADM* advises you to preempt any avoidable hurt by urging you to institute damage control as early as possible in the relationship—not after it's a done deal.

Make Him Yours

HTMADM's goal is to best promote your ability to capture his heart and deliver your Divorced Man as you want him—on his knees.

From the book's instructive question and answer format, to its supporting worksheets, testimonials, and comprehensive lists of tips, you will find that all these elements will facilitate your quest and will help you secure this happy occasion.

THIS BOOK ASSUMES THE FOLLOWING

You are a single woman. Most likely, you've never been married, but then again, you could also be a divorcée, perhaps one with your own children from a prior marriage. (We won't be covering blended family issues in detail in *HTMADM*—that's a whole book in itself and, who knows, perhaps even a sequel to this one.) With all that you have experienced and accomplished at this point in your life you can genuinely admit to being satisfied with yourself. By your reading this book, I can surmise that you are growth oriented and self-aware. You know your uniqueness and how invaluable that is to any Divorced Man you meet. You are actively seeking to better your world. And while you may be content with your life, you also feel it could be enriched with the right man by your side for the long term.

Like most of us, you have survived some romantic highs, but, alas, too many lows. You never stop musing about when this will turn around. You look up to the open heavens and ask, "When will I meet him?" So you persevere from one day to the next, hoping, praying that your question will be answered with "Very soon!" so you can eventually stop talking to the sky, or can at least change the topic of conversation and begin your life as part of a couple.

He is a Divorced Man, or even a serial divorcé. Short of insisting that he whip out his divorce agreement during the first month of dating, you are positive that he is divorced. Warning, warning—do not be fooled. Remember, it's all too easy for him to slip a wedding ring into his pants pocket. A man merely separated from his wife or in the throes of a divorce often has way too much to deal with. I refuse to even entertain the absurd notion of a FateMate dating a married man. He cannot possibly have the wherewithal to love you the way you deserve to be loved. Unless you enjoy your heart being broken, stay far away. Tell him to give you a call *after* the dust settles from his divorce and he is ready to move on. Please note: On average, there is an adjustment period that takes men from two to six years after a divorce, whether they are the leaver or the leavee, before they are able to enter healthy, successful relationships.

And last but not least, if he has children from his earlier marriage, he is decent to them and would not be considered part of the 15 percent of Divorced Men who are labeled deadbeat dads. If he is one of these, a self-respecting FateMate like you certainly wouldn't love him. If he hasn't any children, well then, you'll be able to skip Chapter 10 in this book.

PART II

HIS
EMOTIONAL
LIFE

◆ 4. He Is a Unique ◆ Species

What in the world is going on here?

A Divorced Man, or the prospect of meeting one, has piqued your interest enough for you to pick up this book. You're even wondering if he might be *the one*. You may have just met him, and yet feel as though you've known him your entire life. Or perhaps you have known him for a while and, à la *When Harry Met Sally,* the timing is finally right for you two to get closer. No matter how you've come together, it's both exciting and exasperating. And let's face it, once you get to know your Divorced Man, you find you love him, and yet, you also hate him. And if he hasn't given you any reason to hate him, just give him time and read on.

You may feel he pulled a switcheroo on you. At first, he seduced you with his swaggering charm and his postdivorce zeal for living large. Then, once the relationship became more intimate, he did a 180-degree turn—everything became so heavy. What happened? After all, he looks like all the other men you've dated. He doesn't smell different, dress like an alien, or even speak in tongues. And yet, as you've already noticed, he's the most perplexingly wonderful and altogether different species you've ever known. If men are from Mars, then Divorced Men are from a different galaxy altogether.

For the uninitiated woman who cannot recognize the unique

constitution of the Divorced Man she is dating, both joy and danger lie ahead. His differences are invisible to the naked eye. Unfortunately, we women were not born with the tools to instinctively handle such a rarified creature as he.

> Meet Layla, a stunning, thirty-two-year-old rep for a hot fashion designer. Layla is having the time of her life. Indulging in serial-dating escapades, Layla is the talk of her married friends (whose chatter is perhaps tinged with a wee bit of envy?). When Layla met Don, she was dazzled. He took her to the hippest restaurants and even on a long, steamy weekend in St. Barts where he ordered in perfect French. "At last," she cooed, "a man with the carefree spirit and savoir faire I've always dreamed of." After a few weeks of fantasyland, Don announced that he had a surprise for her; he was taking her to the circus. "How adorable," Layla purred, "I do love the little boy in him." She was, however, totally unprepared to love the little boy with him.

> Before this, Don had never even mentioned his son. And now, out of the blue, she was being introduced to six-year-old Peter, who seemed to need even more time and attention than she did. Late nights at the latest brasseries began to be replaced by drive-through burger joints, allowing more time for picture-book reading sessions.

☞ Reeling & Dealing: With a Divorced Man, what you first see is often not what you get. Instead, it is imperative that you look beyond the obvious. Ask yourself: Underlying his words and actions, what is he really telling you? Or failing to tell you? Cease relying solely on your five senses as they'll get you nowhere fast. Scrutinizing his résumé like a corporate human-resources director won't help much either. To truly understand this man, you will need to fine-tune your ability to read his subtext for the subtle and the not-so-subtle signs.

Don didn't overtly lie or exaggerate. He simply omitted. Or, delayed the truth. As a result, he appeared dishonest to Layla. Certainly, he should have been more forthcoming from the start, but he was scared as he believed this part of his life would frighten Layla away. He was right.

On the other hand, if Layla had honestly wanted a serious relationship, it was her responsibility to seek the truth. Just because Don was a coward, it didn't mean that Layla should be one too. No wonder Don had been unavailable every other weekend. How oblivious could Layla have been? She never pressed for details because she thought his divorce talk would be such a downer in their whirlwind romance. She wanted to see herself only as the sexy, upbeat girlfriend, never the nanny. And since she wasn't getting paid, then, technically, it made her closer to an au pair.

By avoiding the facts and not confronting the realities of the relationship, Layla set herself up for the ultimate downer—the end of her affair. Don's poor handling of the situation was such a devastating blow that it made her realize she would never find everlasting love if she didn't know exactly where her man was coming from or where he wanted to go. From this point on, Layla got wise—she left no question unasked.

That said, it is entirely within your rights to probe. In fact, it is a woman's prerogative, embedded in our DNA. All the FateMates interviewed for *HTMADM* agreed that taking the time to research the reasons for why he got divorced was essential before pledging their love. So, don't you dare think of his divorce as a taboo dialogue. Although society has stigmatized the subject and your Divorced Man doesn't bring it up, it doesn't mean you shouldn't. Inquiring FateMate minds have a right to know. Go ahead. Just do it gently and gracefully.

✐ TIPS: THE DATING GAME

It would be nice to imagine that you could allow your relationship to develop at its own natural pace, then, once you sense he is comfortable, ask him questions related to his past. But that would be suicide *d'amour*. You saw what happened to Layla. What you don't know *can* hurt you. Nope, he very well may be loath to bring up the subject of his divorce, so it's up to you.

To this end, I have devised a list of questions, along with a corresponding schedule, to help you extract the appropriate information from him at the appropriate times in your budding relationship.

Date #1

Consider this date a friendly fact-finding mission. At this point in the relationship, you don't yet know if this man will be meaningful in your life, but just in case, you'll want to collect key information that would affect you as his future FateMate. Begin by only asking questions for which he provides objective answers, sticking to just the facts, as if he were filling out an IRS form. While making the following inquiries and upon receiving his responses, I urge you to play it cool. Remain poised, look keenly interested, and smile. Whether you are relieved to learn that he has one sweet toddler instead of three raucous teenagers with multiple piercings, or alarmed as he informs you that his insidious X lives only a couple of blocks away, do not display your true emotions. They are entirely valid, but does he have to know how you really feel at this early stage? You are not yet involved with this man, so save your raw sentiment for later, when you actually care. Then, there will be plenty of time for you to convey how you feel. I promise.

Questions:

☐ **Are you divorced?**

☐ **For how long?**

☐ **Do you have any children?**

☐ **Where and with whom do they reside?**

☐ **How old are they?**

☐ **How often do you see them?**

Simple and within the realm of politesse. Once you've received your answers, promptly redirect the discussion to a light and breezy subject. "Seen any good movies lately?"

Dates #2, #3, and #4
Have pure, unabashed fun. No mentioning of any weighty divorce topics now.

Dates #5 and Beyond

Once date number five rolls around, hopefully a sense of trust has begun to emerge as you become more intimate. If you've established that you enjoy each other's company and will continue to do so, it's now time to delve deeper.

It's a fine line to cross. You want to know about his past, but you don't want to seem too invasive too early. It is critical that you don't come off like the grand inquisitor. If he perceives that he is being interrogated, he'll be apt to get defensive and be wary of revealing how he truly feels. That means no bombarding him with questions all at one time. Stretch them out over a period of several dates, particularly during loving moments. And please, do not approach him with a printed questionnaire in hand or the next page from this book.

While he may be willing to open up and discuss matters of the heart with you, the following questions may or may not make him uncomfortable. Your job is to read into how he responds, or fails to. Any clues and cues you glean from him will provide you with an indication as to your chances of marrying and staying married to him. Don't be afraid to ask. After all, it's your future we're securing. Make that happy future happen sooner rather than later by asking the questions below.

Questions:

☐ Why did your first marriage end?

☐ Who initiated the divorce?

☐ If it was your X, why did she do so?

☐ If you left her, why did you do so?

☐ Would your X agree with this assessment? (Say this laughingly, throwing back your head in one flippant gesture.) If not, why would she say it dissolved?

☐ What kinds of terms are you and your X now on? Amicable? Cordial? Hostile? Nonexistent?

☐ Why did you marry her?

☐ How would you describe your relationship with your children? (No need to get intense here as you'll probably meet them later and be able to judge for yourself.)

Do you believe him as he answers all of the above? Time will tell. What do you make of his body language? Do you see beads of sweat forming on his palms or forehead? Any squirming in his seat? Clearing his throat? Loosening of his tie? Or is he responding in a genuinely relaxed and thoughtful manner? How he reacts to your questions is a helpful indicator of just how receptive he is to embarking on a life with you.

For him, it is a delicate balance. On the one hand, if he is sincerely ready to start a relationship with you, you need to hear that he has analyzed the demise of his marriage and is ready to take some responsibility for what went wrong. Make sure you hear the words "I did," or "I was." On the other hand, if he puts the blame solely on himself, he paints a pitiful picture: "I was an unappreciative husband . . . an absent father. . . ." You're then apt to think he's a loser still wallowing in regret and promptly lose interest. Or, if he admits to being unfaithful, you might run for the hills, foreseeing that he might do the same to you.

More likely, he'll blame the X. He'll describe her as the devil incarnate who manipulated him into marrying her, robbed him blind, refused him sex, tried to turn the kids against him, a veritable lunatic, all while he was his saintly self. Then again, he might refrain from bad-mouthing her so he doesn't come off as a complete idiot for marrying her in the first place.

Divorced Men who've been active on the dating circuit quickly learn to formulate canned responses that work in allaying their dates' basic concerns. However, these pat answers are rarely the whole truth and often anything but the truth. "My X and I get along famously, really. She's a terrific person." If that's true, then why are they no longer married?

And yet, how he refers to his X is significant. Does he speak lovingly, disrespectfully, or neutrally with appropriate distance? You certainly do not want a Divorced Man who is pining away for his X, nor one still furious with her. A Divorced Man needs to feel indifferent or, at best and on the rarest occasions, friendly toward his X. Only then is he truly ready for you. Otherwise, he enters the relationship with unresolved feelings toward women that will most likely be directed toward you (much more on this in Chapter 6). And come

to think of it, how does he feel about his mother? Oh, forget it—
it's way too complicated. Don't even go there until date number
twenty!

Tit for tat time. If you want him to open up to you, then you too
will have to divulge elements of your past, though best not to give
him a detailed list of all the men you've ever slept with—it always
bites you back. Try going first; it will set the stage for an open
exchange, after which he may be more willing to impart feelings that
he finds so difficult to communicate. If you've never been married,
chances are your serious relationships aren't all that serious com-
pared to his, anyway. Keep this in perspective and share. You've got
nothing to lose and everything to gain.

Ultimately, you need a man who can reflect, learn, live, and
commit to moving toward a better tomorrow. If he's clueless, or
outright refuses to discuss his bygone life, this Divorced Man will
require extreme FateMate guidance in order to come to terms with
his past. After a period of time and several attempts, if he's not moving in the direction of self-awareness, cut your losses and move on.

Don't forget: Never cease continuing to ask follow-up questions
as they arise for you. The more information you gather, the more
heightened your instinctive powers will be. It's called *woman's intu-
ition* and it's yours to tap in to. Remember, men don't have this
innate gift so you're already way ahead of the game.

❖ 5. The Good News ❖

He's everything you've ever wanted. . . .

HE IS EVERYWHERE

The odds are in your favor. With a 50 percent divorce rate, Divorced Men are omnipresent. Tracking them down is also getting easier. Short of lurking around the halls of community-support groups for Divorced Men (these guys can be such a whiny bunch), dating services specializing in the divorced are springing up on the local level. Check your neighborhood listings.

If it's important to you that your Divorced Man be a good father, you'll want to witness him in action. When looking to meet one, try frequenting children's toy or clothing stores on weekends. Alibi: You're buying for your niece or nephew—you can always return it later. Many Divorced Men contemplate meeting women who have children because they think single moms will have a better under-standing of their plight. So you may consider borrowing a niece, nephew, or friend's kid for a weekend movie matinee and see what happens. Caution: Going alone can make you look a tad suspicious.

Another idea is to volunteer for kid-centric community events such as school weekend carnivals. Or perhaps you have a long-lost skill set that suits working with children, like tutoring in math or teaching tennis. How about entertaining them? Does dressing in clown costumes and being jettisoned out of a cannon appeal to you? Balloon sculpting or unicycling? Divorced Men are notorious for spending lavishly at their children's birthday parties.

Other than a dedicated search for Divorced Men, there are the usual ideas and prospective places for meeting any single man. First, envision what kind of mate you would want and what his interests would be. Or select an area that has always interested you and is also one that you would like your partner to be interested in as well. Zero in from there. Academic or hobbyist courses where you study together are excellent choices: "May I borrow your notes?" Lessons in music, sky diving, personal investing, art appreciation—the possibilities are endless. Social-dance class is always a winner, as being held in close proximity can be a good proxy for a relationship. Can he lead? Increasingly, group travel excursions are an ideal outlet for rugged adventurers or culturally curious singles.

Charitable organizations are benefiting from the singles splurge as well. Meeting a man while volunteering for the less fortunate indicates that he may have a compassionate streak. Besides, doing good deeds can enhance your karma. Along these lines, religious community organizations often host singles events. One Divorced Man dared to admit to me that he turned to his church because he discovered that single women of a certain thirty-plus age often seek spirituality as solace in their desperation to meet a man. Yikes, watch out for this guy! Another cunning Divorced Man confessed he'd frequent SmokeEnders meetings because the women were edgy, needy, and orally fixated.

Of course, hang out in the public domain: bookstores, bars, parties, sports events, concerts, art exhibits, and men's clothing stores. Although it seems very 1980s, gyms are still advantageous on many counts. They alleviate stress for you and create a toned body filled with swirling endorphins that make you feel good about yourself. All the while, you get to check out your Divorced Man's body as he gets back into tip-top shape for dating. Plus, for some sports, such as tennis and rock climbing, gyms will frequently match singles into pairs.

Naturally, tell all your friends and relatives with exquisite taste that you are on the prowl. Make sure that your friends tell their friends that they know this fab gal with a particular fondness for Divorced Men who is willing to be set up on blind dates. Ask and ye shall find.

☞ Reeling & Dealing: I've often wondered why newspapers, magazines, and websites don't devote space to what could be a new and exciting section called the "Divorce Announcements." After all, we devour the ever-growing wedding announcements in our local papers even if we don't personally recognize the newly-weds. After scouring the photos, you hone in on the faces of couples who appeal to you, then read on. How did they meet? What college did the bride go to? Was the bride or groom of noted ancestry? Will they be younger or older than you when they tie the knot? We all are vicariously fascinated by reading their love stories.

Similarly, the personals sections in newspapers are increasing as well. Like any such classifieds section in a newspaper, it can be a very profitable business.

So why not have the Divorce Announcements? A kind of marriage obituary, if you will. Wouldn't you like to know which Divorced Men are fresh on the market? Get a heads-up on how handsome he is, his age and profession, and why he divorced? By the way, I'm half joking, half serious. But you get the idea: Wherever you are, Divorced Men can be found.

HE IS THE MARRYING KIND

Divorced Men who entertain the notion of serious relationships typically like the institution of marriage—either that or he's a glutton for punishment. He's *gettable*. Studies show that 75 percent of divorced people remarry within five years, the majority of these second timers being the X-Husbands. Why are Divorced Men more likely to get rehitched more quickly than their Xs? Reason number one: Because they can. Since they tend not to be the custodial parents, they *appear* footloose and fancy free, making dating and remarriage easier. Reason number two: They are considered to be in the prime of their lives longer than women—outrageously unfair, I know. And reason number three: The fact is that married men are known to be happier, healthier, wealthier, and live longer than single men. According to recent research, unmarried men over forty-five years of age are typically recognized as a neurotic, unhappy, and an unhealthy demographic, while single women in the same age range, divorced or never been married, are comparatively much better off emotionally. Not so surprising, is it?

The point is that no one understands the advantages of marriage better than a once-married man. Having been-there-done-that, your Divorced Man appreciates the value of commitment and knows how to live with a woman. Since he has had practice, he is able to morph into the husband role with relative ease. For instance, he knows never to pick a fight with you prior to your hosting a dinner party. He enjoys nurturing and being a provider. Even some household chores will be a breeze for him thanks to his X's previous domestication effort. No more nagging to lower the toilet seat, he's housebroken. He is also more realistic about the amount of emotional work required to maintain a successful relationship, so the second time around he will often try to be more communicative and express himself better.

It is interesting to note that 75 percent of divorces are initiated by the wife. Thus, a man will passively exist in a miserable married state—capable of having sex in this deplorable condition, mind you—rarely ending the marriage *unless* he has someone new to turn to.

☞ Reeling & Dealing: A certain breed of Divorced Man enjoys being married so much that he'll rush into marrying you. *Whoa!* This Divorced Man is t-e-r-r-i-f-i-e-d of being alone. He may never have learned to be single before he was married and is all the more desperate to reattach. He misses the homespun comforts that often accompany marriage. He needs a fix bad. His ability to get intimate quickly seems fearless and takes you by surprise. For instance, he will supply you with the keys to his apartment *before* you even consider hinting at it. You think, "At last, this must be the one," and go with the flow. Revel in feeling flattered, "Hooray, he wants to marry me!", but only for one millisecond, then get over it. Deep down you know something doesn't feel right about this. His anxiety over being single clouds his ability to love you for *you*. Eventually, when he realizes that things got too cuddly too quickly, he'll freak out, just like the majority of men do. But this Divorced Man will crash harder and retreat all the more resolutely. As they say: Easy come, easy go.

Instead, *you* grab hold of the reins. Bring the necessary caution to the romance before his fear and paralysis eventually kick in. Slow him down so you can get to know each other at an organic pace. Temper his behavior by admitting that you're swooning too, but need to take things step by step. Blame your delaying technique on an experience with a past boyfriend if you must supply a reason. By drawing out the courtship phase, you will give him the opportunity to fall in love with you, instead of being enamored of his concept of a wife. Who knows? You may grow to love him too.

An inadvertent bonus: He will experience your deliberately unhurried momentum as a big tease that will make him feel even more determined to win you over. But promise me, no wedding plans with this one until you've dated for nine months (a natural gestation period). Minimum.

He Sticks

If your Divorced Man is a responsible and loving parent, you have a built-in indicator that he is faithful to his family and commitments. For many women, loyalty is a primary factor when selecting a mate. He may start off the relationship posturing as Mr. Happening, but deep down, his sense of duty is strong. Instinctively, you can feel that he's a safer bet than perennial bachelors—and we've all dated too many of them.

☞ Reeling & Dealing: If you are the type who enjoys sitting on pins and needles waiting to see if he'll call after his motorcycle meet on Friday night, or if you get off on not knowing if that sexy waitress at Sunday brunch might be your competition by dinner, in other words, if you are a masochist, then the reliable disposition of the Divorced Man may not be for you. In fact, if you're still hot for rogues who torture you with their bad-boy behavior and infidelities, then *HTMADM* probably isn't for you. But read on anyway to make sure.

> On Layla's previous birthday, her mom, who wants Layla married more than anything else, had a long talk with her daughter. All right, perhaps it was more of a lecture. "Darling, you've been sulking ever since you broke up with Don. As a result, you've gone on a string of dates with lifer-bachelors. Now, I know they can be appealing because they seem freewheeling and tend not to be committed to their pasts the way Don was.

*But, the truth is that they're way too risky as husband
material. I don't care how hunky they are, the divorced
ones may carry some baggage, but who doesn't? After
your Don experience, you now know what's in store
when you date a Divorced Man, so deal with it. If you
want a man devoted to you through thick and thin, and
I do mean your waistline, sylphlike though it currently is,
when the skin around your knees starts to sag and your
eyebrows grow like weeds, I'm really depressing myself
here, the Divorced Man is apt to be 'the one.'"* She
would know; she's been happily married to Layla's stepfather, himself a Divorced Man, for over twenty years.

This is the one time that Layla truly listened to her mom and
went about on her dedicated Divorced Manhunt, the results of
which we'll get to later.

He Now Knows What He Wants

While it would be sheer folly to expect that he has undergone in-
depth analysis and a catharsis, he has presumably devoted some
time to evaluating himself and the reasons for his first marriage failing. If he's been in therapy, this is often an encouraging sign. However, I caution you against men who pay lip service to the analytic
process and never gain a modicum of insight. Suffice it to say that his
divorce was no picnic, so he doesn't want to sustain another one
and he probably can't afford to anyway. Therefore, he will work
harder at his partnership with you. Unlike the first time around,
when his ideas regarding his starter marriage were more unformed
and uninformed, he is presumably a maturer and wiser man who
can now marry for the right reasons. He *now* knows what he wants:
a secure, centered, and loving FateMate he respects—like you.

☞ Reeling & Dealing: He's so set on making this relationship work that he's apt to turn on his automatic pilot. In order to survive the last miserable phase of his marriage, your Divorced Man, like a good Darwinian mammal, evolved the defense mechanism of shutting down his feelings in order to adapt to his disagreeable environment. During this pre–FateMate era, he became *too* adept at going through the motions. He learned how to do the bare minimum of husband niceties for his X, thus placating her and avoiding any potentially unpleasant confrontations.

Such Divorced Men appear to FateMates as wonderfully obedient and duty bound, and they very well can be; however, often they are actually sleepwalking through their husbandly tasks. "Yes, dear . . . whatever you say, dear. . . ." You get the picture. Like an appendix, no longer necessary yet vestiges remain, he may carry over traces of this behavior into your relationship. Sometimes it takes time to identify such subtle insincerities, but you'll recognize them when he claims he has heard you, but his actions reveal he really hasn't.

What about the high-heeled drama that befell Layla's good friend Madeline? Layla and Madeline first met in a yoga class, both struggling to maintain the downward-dog position when Layla suddenly toppled onto Madeline. Ever since that day, every Saturday morning after their yoga meditation, they rush to the café downstairs where they jolt themselves into a high-voltage caffeineated cappuccino craze and share their Divorced Men stories.

It seems that Madeline, a successful art curator approaching forty, is madly in love with her Divorced

Man, Reg, who she has been seeing exclusively for the past year. They spend almost every night together, even when his two teenagers, Iona and Adele, are visiting. At the beginning of the relationship, Madeline secretly applauded Reg's X for domesticating him. "He's so well trained," she would marvel, "when he stays at my apartment, he even takes out the garbage without the slightest peep from me." Then there was that fateful day. One morning Madeline specifically asked Reg not to dispose of that bag by the door—the one with the Manolo Blahnik stilettos she planned to wear after work to a business cocktail party. Reg sweetly "yes-deared" her, kissed her good-bye, and went off to work. On Madeline's way out, she panicked when she saw that the bag by the door was gone. It was too late. Her sexy sandals were already ashes in the incinerator, never to be stepped into again. Madeline began to question how closely Reg actually listened to her.

To obliterate any robotic gestures in your relationship, pay special attention the next time you sense it might happen. You'd be wise to break his habit by catching him in the act, red-handed, or, better yet, before any further harm is done. Sit him down and make sure his attention is concentrated on what you are conveying. Don't let him give you a vacant stare. Get in his face, repeating everything in slow motion as if he needed to read your lips. Your message must sink in, in a deep and meaningful way.

The following may seem harsh, but it works. Compose on paper a pact that declares exactly what he promises to do and not to do in the future. Writing the text together keeps him engaged and holds him responsible for his future actions. It should be a fun activity, yet with serious undertones. "I, [Divorced Man], solemnly swear to never again . . ." In return, you can pledge to do something as well. Maybe concubine for one night? Have him sign the contract, put it in a safe place, and bring it out for I-told-you-so evidence only as needed.

If you are in the more advanced stages of a relationship, do not hesitate to make him pay damages. The following day, Madeline and Reg went on a shopping expedition—starting at the shoe store.

◈ 6. The Not-So-Good ◈ News

But nobody's perfect. . . .

DENIAL

Get ready for heavy-duty doses of this stuff. Divorced Men's revived single status makes them think they are bachelors, just as they were in their premarriage state—but they are far from it. Masquerading as if they are like any other never-been-married man, they are in denial regarding all the traumatic experiences related to their failed marriage: the rage at the X; the grief of separating from the children; the disappointment over the dissolution of the family unit; their financial depletion; not to mention the disillusionment from engaging in the nefarious and treacherous legal machinations of the divorce itself.

Because the pain of facing these matters is so great, Divorced Men resist delving into their emotional world. All too frequently, they prefer to bury their unresolved issues in the deepest recesses of their psyches. Denial allows them to compartmentalize, focusing only on what they want to see, while protecting themselves from the anguishing truth. Divorced Men also fear that expressing their dark emotions will turn you off and that's the last thing they want to do—they want to appear always ready for action—so they repress their negative emotions even more. Unless these outstanding sensations of fury and depression are properly dealt with, they will remain intact, yet hidden, like an angry volcano simmering below the surface, waiting to erupt. After years of smoldering, these suppressed anxieties become all the more grueling to unearth. Fate-Mates, that's where you come in.

Divorced Men in denial waltz into new relationships thoroughly unaware of the havoc they will wreak on unsuspecting FateMates. Unbeknownst to you, the Divorced Man's brewing pain may occasionally leak into your relationship in the form of his moroseness, irritability, defensiveness, or withdrawal. And because he's in denial, he's not likely to be aware of his own emotional transgressions. It will not always be obvious to either of you as to what triggers his mood-altering moments. Observe if he reacts differently after a conversation with the X, or some time with his kids. Driving by a father and son playing ball in their front yard, or hearing the Teletubbies theme song could do it too. As a result, you may find yourself reacting inexplicably sullenly when you experience his mood swinging south.

☞ Reeling & Dealing: Instead of falling prey to his ignorance and brooding, you need to take responsibility for helping him comprehend his hidden nature. You can do this by discovering and uncovering his interior dialogue. Your job is to solve his mystery for him as he'll never be able to do it for himself.

As a first attempt at repairing this particular condition, I recommend proceeding gently, yet proactively. (Hardball tactics may need to be employed later, but we'll get to that soon enough.) Most important, he needs to be able to share his feelings with you in order to get closer. And while a man bellyaching over his first marriage may very well repel you—trust me!—you'll need to be an empathetic listener. Tell him it's essential for you to understand where he's coming from. Let him know that you are there to soothe and coddle him when he needs it. He must come to regard you as such an invaluable and irreplaceable resource that no other woman could supplant you. However, be prepared—the process may require some time.

> *Take, for instance, the example of one bottled-up Divorced Man. He was so emotionally plugged up after his wife callously divorced him that he denied his denial. With almost one year of constant encouragement from his new girlfriend, he eventually grew so proficient at expressing himself that he was compelled to discuss every little thing: his toothbrushing rigor and associated enamel decay; how rain patterns over the past year had adversely affected his sewage system. No topic was too inconsequential for him. This FateMate cursed herself (under her breath, that is) for having cheered him on by telling him that she actually cared to know everything that was on his mind. And yet, in turn, this Divorced Man felt relief from no longer harboring his burdensome feelings and became emotionally emancipated so that he was able to love again. Not much later, this FateMate became his wife. At that point, she finally told him (only in the most loving tone, of course) to shut up. Now that's what I consider a success story: He learns how to express himself, and, as a result, they develop a more intimate rapport, living happily ever after—and then he learns to keep quiet again.*

✐ **TIPS:** <u>ANTIBROODING</u>

Don't let your Divorced Man withdraw into his denial-ridden shell. Now is the time to transform any lingering doubts he may have on moving forward into occasions that will advance your bond as a couple. Sharing your inner thoughts with each other is the best way to become more connected. By establishing yourselves as a two-some, your Divorced Man will feel that his innermost secrets are safe with you.

*1. **Find love in the little things**. Keep him emotionally engaged by connecting over small tasks together: walking the dog, grocery shopping, or reading to each other. Romantic poetry like Shakespeare's love sonnets works best, but even the newspaper's op-ed page can do the trick. Though it may sound mundane, you're actually sharing life-building experiences.*

*2. **Invite fun and hope into his life so there's always a treat to look forward to**. Consider life as a continual celebration. Attend parties, go out dancing, pack a picnic, travel to new destinations, take a class together—anything to get him out of the house and out of his rut. Arrange the plans yourself; don't wait for him to do it. (But then don't complain that he doesn't make plans. Instead, be thankful that you're in charge and get to do what you want to do.)*

*3. **Avoid emotional triggers that remind him of his past marriage**. Make the most of your child-free time together by selecting romantic vacation spots for couples only, restaurants that are intimate and dimly lit, neighborhoods or territories that are new to the two of you, or movies that are R-rated and beyond.*

*4. **Discuss your dreams and goals**. Building toward a future is part of setting up your foundation as a partnership; and creating a pos-*

itive foundation from the get-go will be that much harder to destroy later on. How do you see yourselves living years from now? Where will it be? In what climate or environment? Next to your family and friends or far away from them? With or without children? What will you be doing there? Working? Community or charity work? Along these lines, do you have similar financial aims? What will your lifestyle be like? What else would you like to aspire toward and accomplish? This is also an invaluable way to assess whether you both share the same aims for a harmonious life together.

*5. Start creating customs, routines, rituals, and myths early in the relationship to establish your **coupleness**. These can be small, incremental additions to your existing life together. Perhaps you're doing many of these already. For example:*

- **A manageable *custom* would be to spend Sunday-night dinners out at your favorite Italian restaurant, or to take an adult-education class together each semester.**

  I know a couple who took weekly tango lessons early in their relationship as a way of making sure they scheduled fun time together. In effect, they were developing their own mating dance and custom. Lo and behold, their first dance at their wedding was a tango done to perfection.

- **A *routine* like preparing his coffee just the way he likes it every morning, or kissing each other every time you say good-bye, is a daily gesture that takes minimal effort, but has a major impact.**

- A *ritual* could be a champagne toast celebrating every job promotion, pay raise, or job change.

- *Myths* are the stories that couples repeat to themselves and to others that epitomize who they are as a partnership.

Everyone knows that Madeline and Reg met sharing a taxi one rainy morning on their respective ways to work. The way they tell it at dinner parties is that they enjoyed each other's company during the thirty-minute cab ride so much that they both skipped work and spent the day chatting in a coffee shop. It was love at first sight. Their punch line: Thank god for New York City traffic!

- Myths may be factual or even embellished.

I distinctly recall it differently. When Madeline first called me in an excited flurry after she met Reg, she said that after stepping out of the cab, they exchanged good-byes and went their separate ways. But then, a few days later, at her desk, she received a call from him asking her to lunch. They set a date for the following week.

Real or surreal—does it really matter? Their public story creates a mythic "it's destiny" aura to their meeting.

6. Remember the power of the written word. If he has trouble expressing himself orally, have him put it down on paper. If this proves to be too difficult, write down your own fears and read them to him: fear of not being loved, of being alone, of being left, of no longer being desirable, of flying, of washing dirty dishes, etc. You can choose to discuss or not discuss what you've both written. The sheer act of communicating feelings, whether spoken or on paper, has a liberating, antibrooding effect. Keep in mind that men like bullet points.

Having confidence in yourself on your quest to open him up will put you in the driver's seat. Think about it another way: How healthy could a relationship possibly be if neither of you is making the effort to dig deeper? Ever witness a couple in a restaurant, at a nearby table, eating the entire meal in silence? Do you want that to be you? Need I say more?

INVISIBLE EGO WOUNDS

After you get him emotionally engaged in the relationship and out of his mopey ways, you'll need to revive him as you would a victim who has suffered a near-death trauma. His experiences may have left him feeling the loss of a more innocent view of the world, his wallet, and, while he'll be loath to admit it, his masculinity.

This means you'll want to be generous in rebuilding any post-divorce damaged self-esteem. You'll be able to resuscitate his spirit and bolster his wounded ego by administering the demonstrative techniques that follow. It's the ol' nurture versus nature duality: If you nurture him well, you can shape his nature.

☞ Reeling & Dealing: The section below can be difficult to digest. These surefire ego boosters will most likely appear a tad retro to the modern FateMate, but like all time-tested classics, they still work. It's interesting that we often forget how easy it is to please. Could it be because the steps to take are so simple and intuitive? Or because it's what our mothers always told us to do?

✐ **TIPS:** REBUILDING HIS SELF-ESTEEM
Give him the incentives he needs to feel worthy of being your man.

1. Treat him like a king. Pay homage and cater to him as it suits your schedule and mood. Recite "Can I get you anything, dear?" queries as necessary, and even when not necessary. It sets the proper tone.

2. Create a harmonious atmosphere in his kingdom and yours. You want to motivate him to spend more intimate time with you. Have his favorite things readily available, plus extra niceties such as candles, wine, etc. to set a romantic ambience in the home. Should you be home before him, have his favorite snacks or beverages prepared. Don't forget to ease the television out of your lives. It zaps energy and precious time away from loving.

3. Be his love slave. Tell him you're his as you physically express devotion in everything you do. Give him lots of hot sex to remind him of why he can't get enough of you. Constantly fondle, caress, stroke, etc. Offer massages, by you or by a professional masseuse. Furnish him with seemingly spontaneous love taps and kisses every time you pass him—but no smothering, please.

4. Speak affectionately with keen interest and respect. Any statements that positively reinforce his ego are your friends. Your conversations should be sprinkled with darling, baby, honey, whatever terms of endearment feel good to you and have the desired effect on him. If you call him pet names enough, it eventually becomes second nature and sets the emotional state for all encounters. In other words, he becomes your darling for real. You don't have to wait to feel the emotion first, just start the affectionate name-calling today. Also, show interest in all that he does. "How was work today, dear?" Remain tuned in to his response even if it bores you into oblivion. Last, praise him. His negotiation skills, wine connoisseurship, penis size, driving ability, etc.

5. Let him think that you accept him as he is, warts and all. At least for now. You and I both know that his warts are objectionable, and he too will come to understand this if he allows his foibles to flourish. (See "Let's Play Hardball" in Chapter 13.)

6. Cherish the relationship, making it a top priority. Take the time to exhibit little love gestures for each other daily so the relationship always feels special.

> For example, my cousin's husband used to be abrupt and coarse; how she tolerated him, we'll never know. But years later, after doting on him unconditionally, he's a new man and we call him Mr. Miracle Whipped to Perfection. He even wakes up thirty minutes early every morning to prepare his wife's favorite fruit smoothie so that it's ready for her as she stumbles out of bed. He says love changed him. Not his love for her, but her love for him.

7. Deploy optimism and humor. An engaging attitude puts you in control. Don't lose this vantage point.

Disclaimer: My own Divorced Man laughed uproariously when he read the above, demanding why the doctor can prescribe the medicine, but can't swallow it herself. Well, there's no use pretending—it ain't easy and I'm only human. But, ever the test dummy, I've been following my own advice and taking the daily dosage, dispensing the sweets to my Divorced Man, and eureka—it's been working wonders.

However, if, after a goodly amount of time, the above compassionate route doesn't make your Divorced Man yours and he remains in a denial-laden funk, you'll need to embark on harsher maneuvers. Basically, he needs you to snap him out of it, so you'll have to do whatever it takes. Be sympathetic, yet firm. You'll probably have to employ a tougher tone. He should be able to share his feelings with you, but after a point, enough is enough and he must learn to stop wallowing. If he doesn't, *you'll* be the one wallowing in his misery. Continue to be empathetic with his saga, but not embroiled in it. After all, are you going to let him bring you into his musty, moody, immobilized, divorce-infested world? Let his kvetching bring you down? Hell, no! You are not responsible for his marital mistakes and therefore should not bear the brunt of his negativity.

I mean, come on, who hasn't emotional scars from past relationships? And while yes, the Divorced Man's wounds may be deeper, haven't we all survived life's upsets and still chosen to move onward? And here we are ready to try again. FateMates tend to be much more resilient than our Divorced Men, so you will need to impart that strength to him.

Delicately, inform him that he is not allowed to blame, whine, or pout in your presence. Just as psychiatrists say that bringing home work-related stresses will suffocate any healthy relationship, divorce spillover in a new relationship, or even an old one, for that matter, is a no-no. Contrary to what used to be the conventional wisdom of spewing forth one's anger and grief, psychologists now believe that too much venting is actually harmful, as it perpetuates the pain and is an obstruction that keeps the victim from moving on. For most Divorced Men, time alone doesn't heal wounds, rather, it magnifies and perpetuates them.

If he indulges in this repetitive sob song, calmly explain, in so many words, "This is not new information. I've heard this story before and I am not sure what you expect to gain by droning on. I realize it is difficult ending a part of your life and beginning a new one, but it is also exciting, and if you want to move ahead, we can do that together." Don't let him detect any sarcasm in your voice that may inadvertently seep in.

In any case, his divorce should never be associated with failure. A man often feels like an emotional wreck if his marriage didn't work, but the reality is that exiting from an unhappy marriage is a success. He may bemoan, "Could I have saved the marriage? Did I make the wrong decision in divorcing my X?" While it's necessary for him to be mulling over these questions so that he can advance with you—enough already! Self-flagellation is entirely counterproductive. Besides, staying in a failed marriage would have been a wretched idea. Is he such a denial junkie that he even becomes nostalgic for a past that he has forgotten made him miserable?

You'll also need to bring a new and upbeat perspective to his situation. Don't pathologize divorce as a negative crisis, which our culture tends to do; instead, show him that change can mean a better future filled with newfound hope. Spin it as a positive transition. Projecting optimism, assure him that it takes much strength and courage to make the journey, but it's worth it and he's the man to do it. That you are the woman to do it is implied. Celebrate as if it's all part of an exhilarating rebirth for him. Divorce is not just an ending, it is also a new beginning, a new life, a new love, and sometimes even a new wardrobe.

Remind him that in days of yore, when the life expectancy was thirty-five, a person was stuck with only one partner their whole life. Is he pining away because of an antiquated notion? How passé. In this constantly evolving world, with our increased life spans, endless possibilities, and freedom of choice, divorce almost becomes inevitable. Point out his friends who are listlessly going through the motions in their first marriages, yet are secretly salivating over the chance to start afresh with a FateMate. Now, your Divorced Man has the good fortune to begin anew. How lucky he is!

And for god's sake, don't pity and indulge him when he reverts to obsessing. I know you don't want to appear insensitive, but you are not his caretaker. A nurse tends to her patient's wounds until he is able to stand on his own and, with his strength regained, is promptly released from the infirmary. Once revived and acclimated back into society, your Divorced Man becomes the man you always dreamed of—insightful, strong willed, ready for a loving relation-ship—except he eventually dumps you for a gal who doesn't remind him of his miserable postdivorce slump. Instead, she is scin-tillating and titillating, just like you used to be. Let her be you.

GUILT

Divorced Men who are still stuck like fossils in their predivorced past typically live with guilt—if you can call that *living*. While some Divorced Men are more prone to this than others, they all suffer from it to some degree. He may experience feelings of guilt stem-ming from possible marital indiscretions, over not being emotionally available to his wife and ultimately driving her to becoming an X, over disappointing his children, from being in denial of all his trans-gressions, or even subconsciously feeling guilty that he's cheating on his X by having a relationship with you. What's a FateMate to do?

Festering guilt will force him to hitherto unforeseen heights of unawareness, and its manifestations come in all shapes and sizes. For instance, he refuses to spend Thanksgiving without his X. Or take a vacation without his children. And why is it that five years after the divorce, he still pays his X's cell phone bill every month?

Of course, he promises you that he no longer has feelings for the X, but then why does he allow her to take delight in abusing him? When she needs something from him, why does he jump at her beck and call? As deranged as it may be, does he find excuses to contact her? Due to his guilt, he will unwittingly (because his wits are obviously not always about him) let the X and the children get away with murder. They will surely take advantage of it, that is, until you set him straight.

> *Just as Madeline and Reg were getting serious, he started visiting his former home each week, claiming he needed to browse through old files he still kept in the basement. Seizing the opportunity, the X would ask him to do plumbing handiwork while he was there. Or else, she threatened, there could be an "accidental" flood and his papers would be ruined. Without batting an eye, he complied. Instead of spending precious afternoons with Madeline, he was repairing his X's old rusty pipes. Playing the part of the permanently embittered victim, as though she was Oscar material, the X relished the opportunity to make him pay up any way she could.*

☞ Reeling & Dealing: Nothing will infuriate you more than his inability to be rational. When faced with relics from his past, your otherwise intelligent Divorced Man becomes a pea brain. During these moments *you* need to be the logical, thinking half of your couple. Even if this is not your natural disposition, you must locate and strengthen the reasonable side of your personality if you want to deal with him correctly. Err on the side of overcommunicating to get him to understand that there is too much madness in his method, how it is unhealthy for all, and how you refuse to live with it.

In the above example, Reg was subconsciously attempting to make amends with the X for his guilt over instigating the divorce. Even though the X also wanted the divorce, which was as amicable as they come, Reg couldn't help but take a decade-long guilt trip. Why so long? Guilt tends to work in mysteriously lingering ways.

> *After Madeline's tantrums got her nowhere, and as she felt more confident in the relationship, she smartened up. Her remedy was simple: The X's abode was not to be used as a storage bin. Reg must move his files out of the X's basement and into his new home or rent a self-storage unit. In fact, after this episode was tidily concluded, entering the X's interior space was to be avoided at all costs. Why risk his getting all misty eyed at passing his favorite armchair? Even when he was picking up or dropping off the kids and needed to use the bathroom, she suggested he hold it in.*

FateMate, your mission is the same as Madeline's: to reduce the control the X has over your Divorced Man's life. If he complains that the rental unit is too expensive, explain that this investment is a mere pittance to be paid in exchange for your love. If he disagrees, then he's not ready to move on—but you should.

✐ TIPS: DEPROGRAMMING HIM

Guilt requires strong measures. Unless you deprogram him, he'll continue to conjure up cockamamy alibis that keep him tied to his past. Though it may be evident to everyone that his marital situation has changed, he might be slow to internalize it. Always assume that your Divorced Man doesn't even realize how strong a hold the X continues to have over him. In fact, he probably didn't even know there was a problem till you came along. Sad but true—a legal divorce is often faster and easier to obtain than an emotional divorce.

In general, guilt has your Divorced Man so mired in his old nasty habits that he literally cannot see alternative ways of responding to the X. As a result, he cannot openly approach his problems with the resolve to resolve. That's where you come in. The concept is to show your Divorced Man that he's been stuck in an emotional morass and needs to relearn ways of acting and reacting to his X. To protect your terrain as a couple, set boundaries by using these deprogramming tips:

1. Delay his responses to the X. When the X presents a challenge, have your Divorced Man delay his response to her. He'll get back to her in his own time, after he's consulted with you for out-of-the-box FateMate solutions, has had ample time to mull over assorted ways of reacting, and when he's good and ready. In the meantime, together walk through other possible scenarios, step by step, on how to deal with her. Once you agree on an approach, only then may he reply. For example:

Late last April, Reg's X telephoned in hysterics. She claimed she needed money for Iona's second month of summer camp ASAP or else they would cancel her first-month slot. She then put thirteen-year-old Iona on the phone who awkwardly said that her mom was suddenly insisting that she go to the second camp session, and that it was okay with her. Now, normally Reg would have deferred to the X's judgment and immediately cut a check to the camp, but this time he knew better and told her he'd call her back.

He turned to Madeline with that "What am I to do?" look on his face, which usually sends her into spasms, but this time propelled her into high FateMate gear. "Funny," she recollected, "Iona had previously voiced her excitement in hanging out with her friends at home for August, and your X never wanted her to attend the second month of camp—why now?" Aha! The X's ulterior motive suddenly hit Madeline. The X must want a cleared-out household so she could romance her new boyfriend without distraction, as Iona's older sister Adele was on a teen tour the entire summer. No wonder Reg sensed discomfort in Iona's voice; she felt she was being ousted from her own residence. (Congratulations to any FateMate who gets her Divorced Man to such a heightened state of awareness and sensitivity!)

*Madeline and Reg talked through several possible sce-
narios of response, all with the goal of seeking what was
best for his daughter. They both decided that rather
than genuflect to the X's manipulation, Reg would first
discuss with Iona the option of her staying in camp for
six weeks instead of the originally agreed-upon four
weeks or the X's proposed eight, then consider accompanying her dad and Madeline on a ten-day white-
water rafting and hiking trip. Reg called Iona, and Iona
was thrilled. Confident, with Iona's enthusiasm still
ringing in his ears, Reg practiced with Madeline what
he would say to the X. They even anticipated her
objecting retorts as they acted out a homemade script:
"When the X says this, you say that . . . ," etc. Reg
then called his X back, informed her of the new game
plan, and let her know that if she was interested, she
would be responsible for paying for the extra two weeks
of camp that she had orchestrated. Madeline called
the camp, and of course they would be delighted to
have Iona for six weeks instead of four.*

Without your input and guidance, this last-minute phone call
would probably have caused a passive, knee-jerk submission from
Reg. Or if he protested without a well-thought-through remedy,
Reg and his X's exchange would have turned into a shouting
match with the usual recriminations back and forth, and an
unhappy thirteen-year-old listening in.

By encouraging your Divorced Man to take his time with his
response and walk through various scenarios, he will be able to
turn any episode to his advantage and yours, set a good example

for his child, and learn how to deal with future situations that are all too likely to occur. This method may seem somewhat tyrannical and time consuming, but he needs your creative input; otherwise, he'll lapse back into his old dismal ways.

2. Reorient him by using a secret code. Once he comprehends his old pattern and tells you that he wants to break it, try this: Agree on a special word, phrase, gesture, or facial expression that will have a specific meaning recognized only by the two of you. This secret code, when executed by you, will serve to notify him that he is drifting into his old ways, and, ideally, will cause him to stop dead in his tracks so that no further harm is done. For instance, had Madeline felt Reg regressing into his autopilot "Yes, dear" manner before he had mindlessly thrown her shoes into the incinerator, she could have immediately detonated the secret code and salvaged the sandals. As your Divorced Man hears your special mantra, or sees the coded gesture, with practice it should serve to intercept and halt his involuntary switch into default X mode. Instead of leading him back to his old ways, it should propel him straight into clarity and your arms.

3. Recall all. To sever him from his X customs, you will need to regularly remind him of his noxious bond with his past. FateMates, always keep in your head a running list of his transgressions. Or, if this idea seems to be a karmic waste to you, commit them to paper privately. Going forward, there will be times when he denies that he has had any inappropriate attachments to the X—as if you could possibly make it all up. So, lest he forget, you be the one to remember. When you feel more secure in your relationship, and he pulls another Divorced Man doozie, you may need to play the list back to him. At this point in your relationship, flooding him with *examples of his own lunacy should start to make him cringe and he will finally get the point.*

Again, try to talk about his co-dependent behavior with his X by using humor so he can begin to laugh at himself, thus making it easier for him to detach and ultimately break free. Hopefully, one day, when the X performs yet another dastardly deed, something will snap in your Divorced Man and he'll undergo a cathartic experience that will finally allow him to view her for who she truly is—your nemesis. Either that *or* he'll finally realize that he has more to gain by pleasing you than by pleasing his X, especially since you're the one he's bedding.

The key to permanently modifying his behavior is to retrain him by using the above tips while positively reinforcing his good actions. (Refer to "Tips: Rebuilding His Self-Esteem," found earlier in this chapter.) Alternate between hot and cold, though mostly staying hot toward him. Therefore, when delivering the above stricter measures, pepper your verbal punches with "Darling, you're so much sexier when you stand up to her," and the like. Every so often, it's okay to throw him a bone. This way, he is on his haunches, conditioned to wait in hope for his master's reward.

Separation Anxiety

Even though he may have been divorced for some time, there is a good chance that he hasn't yet emotionally weaned himself from his X and, as a result, imposes her presence upon you. If your Divorced Man is still on the rebound (which in Divorced Man-speak can mean years longer and many relationships after his first postdivorce romance), he is apt to become both fascinated and enthralled by anything that appears to be the opposite of his X. If she was a housewife, you are a working girl; if she loved meat and potatoes, you're a health-food enthusiast. Yet, he may simultaneously be distrustful of you for the very same reason that he is attracted to you—because you *are* so refreshingly different from the X.

And if you're not so different from the X—*watch out!* Inevitably, you will remind him of the X (who ended up bringing misery into his life), who probably reminded him of his mother anyway (who brought him into a life of misery). Or maybe he felt snookered into or burned by his last marriage, so he's distrustful of your marital designs and fearful of making the same mistake twice. This man may have a lifelong history of not separating from the women in his life. As a result, he will have a difficult time coming together with you.

You can tell if he possesses this condition when he initiates an argument. Does he mistakenly imbue you with negative character-istics that are more appropriately attributable to his wretched X? (Projecting his X's positive traits onto you is rarely a problem.) He'll erroneously finger your perfectly honorable FateMate intentions through his discolored X-ray lens.

> As Layla confided to Madeline during one of their post-yoga, caffeine-filled gab fests, "Maddy, I think I'm inter-ested in this guy Craig. He's sensitive and intelligent, but when I do anything that remotely reminds him of his X, it's dangerous. In his mind, I immediately embody all her evils, every reason for why he despised her. If I am occasionally too tired to have sex, he grumbles, 'You're just like my X, cold-hearted.' If I ask him not to drop his dirty underwear on the floor, he replies that I'm just as neurotic as the X and that next I'll start throwing the things he dropped into the garbage to punish him, just like she did. I used to not be able to foresee when he

would conjure up her spirit, but now I see his patterns,
though it doesn't make it any easier for me."

Sound vaguely familiar? I can just see the chorus of knowing nods
from FateMates around the world.

Madeline, as always, was able to cut right to the heart
of the problem. "He's obviously displacing the unre-
solved anger he has toward her onto you. Next time
you're together, point it out immediately, as soon and
as often as it happens." Evidently, Madeline's therapy
was kicking in.

The following week Madeline could hardly breathe
through the deep-relaxation portion of her yoga class,
so eager was she to hear how her advice had worked.

Layla filled her in. "Nothing against your advice, honey,
but it was a disaster. He refused to accept any part of
what I was saying. He claimed that he had been over
his X for years and that I was the one with deep-rooted
feelings of inadequacy and was unable to accept help-
ful criticism."

Madeline gave her friend a shoulder to cry on, even
though Layla was laughing. "How did I respond? I threw
his dropped things on top of the garbage, of course,
just like he told me his X used to, and left the relation-
ship for good."

☞ Reeling & Dealing: His convoluted notions can impede your
progress. First and foremost, he must recognize that you are not
her. You are uniquely you. When he tells you, "You're just like my

X," or "You're not enough like my X," sit him down and inquire, "Excuse me, but who is it you are speaking to?" Say it sweetly and innocently so it doesn't further invoke his ire, but instead, gives him pause. Don't expect him to immediately respond, "I am so sorry, darling. I misplaced my anger at my X onto you. It will never happen again." A grunt or a nod that he acknowledges your message will have to suffice until he stops this unappealing habit forever.

Inform him that there will be no comparing and contrasting; it is destructive, not a positive addition, to the relationship. Explain how the synapses in his mind immediately time-travel back to the X, with all her miserable associations. Describe how he misinterprets your words and actions that have nothing whatsoever to do with the X. To assuage his fears of your morphing into the X, explain that you had a very different intention than he wrongly imagined and then proceed to describe it in detail. Where and when appropriate, utilize the tips for deprogramming him as described earlier in this chapter.

Any misplaced misgivings he has from his past relationships with women will feel like a direct affront to you until you manage to not take them personally. Easier said than done, I know. Remember, it's nothing against you; he's just fighting demons from his past. To avoid getting sucked into his vicious cycle, try to make light of it as much as possible. Lift it to the realm of the impersonal, where it belongs.

Just because the X is a psychological hazard to your romance, be careful not to relegate yourself to being the opposite of her, hoping he will love you more this way. Whereas the X was controlling and maniacal, you may decide to be predominantly footloose and fancy free. The point is that you must be true to yourself. Being laissez-faire is only a part of your multifaceted nature. Remember why he originally fell for you? Because you were easy-going as well as feisty, determined, hilarious, brainy, artistic, etc. Don't suppress the fullness of your personality, thinking you should appear as the other extreme of his X. After all, he's only telling you one side of his story with her. Your relationship cannot be an honest one if you are not being yourself; and consequently, you will not be able to receive what you need from the relationship to make it a satisfying one for you in the long run.

If he persists in projecting past sentiments onto you, over time you may begin to understand why his X was an out-of-control lunatic—because he turned her into one. The same way it could happen to you. What FateMate wouldn't go nuts dating a man who accused her of things that had nothing to do with her?

✂ WORKSHEET: IS HE READY TO MOVE FORWARD?

As a result of not thoroughly separating from the X, his *distrust o'meter* can swing off the charts. By answering the questions in the accompanying checklist, you'll be able to gauge whether he's distrustful of you or is ready to become yours. Reply *yes* or *no* to the following questions:

☐   1. Has he introduced you to his friends?

☐   2. Has he introduced you to his children?

☐   3. Has he introduced you to his mother?

☐   4. Does he remain calm and natural when you ask him questions about his X?

☐   5. Does he remain calm and natural when you ask him questions about his kids?

☐   6. Is he no longer in love with the X?

☐   7. Is he no longer enraged by the X?

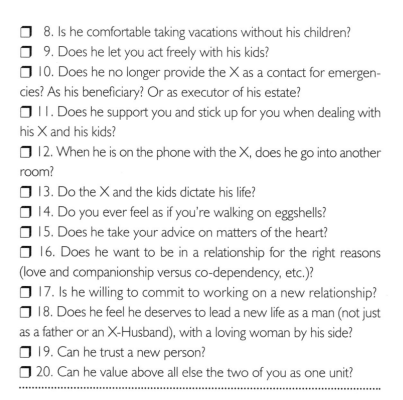

☐ 8. Is he comfortable taking vacations without his children?

☐ 9. Does he let you act freely with his kids?

☐ 10. Does he no longer provide the X as a contact for emergencies? As his beneficiary? Or as executor of his estate?

☐ 11. Does he support you and stick up for you when dealing with his X and his kids?

☐ 12. When he is on the phone with the X, does he go into another room?

☐ 13. Do the X and the kids dictate his life?

☐ 14. Do you ever feel as if you're walking on eggshells?

☐ 15. Does he take your advice on matters of the heart?

☐ 16. Does he want to be in a relationship for the right reasons (love and companionship versus co-dependency, etc.)?

☐ 17. Is he willing to commit to working on a new relationship?

☐ 18. Does he feel he deserves to lead a new life as a man (not just as a father or an X-Husband), with a loving woman by his side?

☐ 19. Can he trust a new person?

☐ 20. Can he value above all else the two of you as one unit?

If your Divorced Man is the trusting sort, capable of starting a life with you, your answers should read: *yes* for questions one to eleven, *no* for questions twelve to fourteen, and *yes* for questions fifteen to twenty. Responses that diverge from these may cause you to reflect on whether or not he can be committed to you—at this point. Isolate these specific issues and watch to see if they improve over time.

If you cannot answer some of the above, don't be discouraged; you may be in the earlier stages of your relationship, so refer back to this list periodically until the response is clear in your mind. To be safe, I recommend not getting 100 percent attached to your

Divorced Man too early. Your objectivity in assessing whether he's capable of self-awareness and transformation requires that you keep a slight distance. And if you are stymied by some of the above questions and not sure where this relationship is going, as a last resort ask him point blank: "Are you capable of trusting and loving me?" Observe his response vigilantly.

To combat his distrust, you will have to show him that you are a safe and nonthreatening haven. But it will take time and patience to melt his distrust into trust. When appropriate, use kindness, honesty, and levity, within the right environment, to accomplish this. To keep yourself interested during his tedious transformation, remind yourself that it is only temporary.

Throughout the process, never stop asking yourself if he is capable of analyzing his past and moving on to enjoy his newfound freedom in loving you. It will take much of his strength and courage—yours too, by the way—to honestly confront why his marriage faltered. By the end of this exploratory work, you will be able to draw him out of his past and show him the benefits of moving on—namely, *you*. Your Divorced Man will feel as though a heavy weight has been lifted off his shoulders, leaving him free to love you all the more for it.

◈ 7. Sex: ◈
Redefining Kinky

Your Divorced Man is hungry for love. Which meal plan did he
sign up for: the Smorgasbord or the No-Dessert Option?

THE SMORGASBORDER

Sexually starved during his last years of marriage, this type of
Divorced Man craves consuming. The heartier the meal, the better.
He also needs to strut his stuff up and down the buffet line to survey
the tantalizing selection. To him, diet is a four-letter word. He'll sam-
ple every dish. This makes him feel cocky again. Desperate to feel
desired after his conjugal loss, the Smorgasborder engages in sexca-
pades that bolster his wounded ego. You may find him to be
promiscuous and even experimental, particularly if he entered a
monogamous marriage at a young age and feels it's time to make up
for missed opportunities.

His mind always wanders to the topic of sex. While all dating
men experience the third-date dilemma, "Will she or won't she
have sex with me on the third date?," this Divorced Man also con-
templates a third-date dilemma all his own: "Tonight, do I or don't I
inform her that I have children? And if I do, will that diminish my
chances of having sex with her?" Certainly!

For the gonad-charged Divorced Man, having sex means he can
be intimate without having to talk about his feelings. This phase of

his, ahem, maturation, can continue for some time depending on how much he relishes his regained bachelorhood.

☞ Reeling & Dealing: As long as you are not at physical risk, and do not feel compromised in any way—go for it! But remember, even nice men who have been married for the majority of their adult lives can contract sexually transmitted diseases. As Mae West so wryly put it, "A good man is hard to find, but a hard man is even better." Why not enjoy it while it lasts? While you may be assessing him as a future husband, the Smorgasborder is checking you out as a future bed partner. For now, let him. The Smorgasborder needs to feel potent again, and your FateMate love can make his testosterone flow. This guy likes to be massively stroked psychologically and physically—so do it.

A clever way to get under this man's skin is to get him physically addicted to you. Start with a simple affectionate gesture like backscratching or massaging. Then, as you two get more intimate, sleeping together often works in your favor. Did you ever get so used to sleeping with someone that when you spent a night apart, your body went into withdrawal, tossing and turning? Get his body habituated to your physical presence. Let his body's memory crave you.

If you're having a hot affair with a Smorgasborder, continue to let him revel in his newfound sexual freedom until it's run its course. Eventually, after he has romped sufficiently, this Divorced Man should miss the emotional connection and loving touch of a marriage. As his sex drive normalizes and the bravado wanes, look beyond your lusty chemistry to make sure you can relate on other important levels: character, value systems, hobbies, intellectually, culturally, DVD collections, etc. These compatibilities should begin to take on greater importance in your relationship without diminishing your active sex life. All the while, be by his side pumping him up, assuring him that he's a sex god and nobody does it better. You know the drill. Once he's ready to let his Dionysian self-image slide, you'll be there by his side and he'll be able to get more genuine with you. Or not . . .

> *Enter Peter. When Layla met him, she was still reeling from the Don debacle and asked Peter all the tough questions upfront. This led to her knowing right off the bat that he had no kids, although he wanted them (they all say that at first), and was madly in love with Layla's freewheeling lifestyle and sensuality. Peter wanted to make up for the decade he'd lost in a sexually unsatisfying monogamous marriage. Having been divorced only six months and loving it, he declared that two-person sex no longer appealed to him.*

> *While Layla really thought Peter was a hot number and, in general, she was sexually adventurous, she had no interest in group groping. However, being a wise young woman about town, she was perfectly willing to accept Peter's under-the-covers preferences—virtually, that is. She showed him how adept she was at exploring fantasy worlds with her Scheherazade-like powers of storytelling during coitus. Peter appreciated her talent. Their sex was frequent and fabulous, with a bedroom populated by the imagined presence of movie stars and other attractive folks seen at restaurants or clubs. So much so that their sex life took on a life of its own, eventually crowding out other more routine ways of communicating.*

Layla was happy to continue in this vein for quite some time, but when Peter insisted on introducing her twenty-five-year-old assistant into the mix . . . well, the bedroom became much too packed. Peter didn't understand Layla's refusal, and wanted to know how, in her eyes, he had changed from a stud to a dirty old man overnight.

It wasn't that Layla was getting bored with all those make-believe people and games, it was that sex had replaced the promise of true intimacy. After several months of trying, he just wasn't able to go there, and the fact was that they had little else in common. Exit Peter.

THE NO-DESSERT OPTION

This Divorced Man is so plagued by the past that he has trouble enjoying himself in the moment. Divorce trauma has ravaged his self-esteem and therefore his appetite, leading him to gorge on all-natural crunchy ingredients, such as guilt, denial, and distrust, found in the previous chapter. Indulge in dessert? Never! Too rich for the senses and way too pleasurable. We recently discussed the fact that if your Divorced Man has not properly separated from his past, then repressed thoughts of the X may involuntarily penetrate his subconscious. *Penetrate*—how appropriate a term; she will rear her ugly head, metaphorically, that is, as he's penetrating you.

It's sad but true—everything surrounding the X in your life with a Divorced Man translates to unsexy. This means that you will have to try ultrahard to instill passion, especially when the X intrudes. And intrude she will. Men who have not resolved the issues with their past may subliminally bring all the X-driven neuroses into the bedroom, where it can interrupt your lovemaking. Room for the three of you on your mattress? No way.

The X's ghost barging into Mr. No-Dessert Option's bedroom may manifest itself in either coitus interruptus where he loses his erection or cannot reach orgasm, or he'll revert back to sexual patterns such as formulas and/or fantasies that he deployed over the last few years of marriage when his relationship with the X was on the outs and sex with her was not particularly pleasurable. At that time your Divorced Man would increasingly rely on his favorite sexual supplements in order to get turned on and perform successfully. Formulas and fantasies became a foolproof habit. If it could work with the X during those trying times, it'll work on you while he's nervous about his postdivorce sexual performance. And if he's thoroughly repressed and too afraid to share his flights of fancy with you, masturbation might be his activity of choice. That's ostensibly one on a mattress. What a turnoff.

Additionally, Divorced Men are often embarrassed on reentering the singles sex scene. They are older, possibly feeling not as virile or sexy as they used to, and are accustomed to appearing naked for only one woman, their former wife. And let's face it, with men, either they can get it up or they can't—there's no faking it.

> *When Madeline first met Reg, she felt she had died and flown straight to single woman's heaven. He was bright, funny, and published fine-art books. She knew he had just suffered through a wicked divorce, but thought that their special compatibility, mixed with eroticism, would triumph. One Saturday after yoga, Madeline burst into tears. She confided in Layla that after thinking she had found her soulmate, there still*

was one obstacle: Their sex life was sorely lacking. For such a creative man, Reg was uncharacteristically formulaic in bed. And to top it off—which he apparently couldn't—Reg was having trouble maintaining his erections.

The other night he had finally been able to talk about the problem. He admitted that during the last five years of his marriage, he and his wife had stopped having intercourse. It seems that whenever he made overtures, his wife would admonish him for one bogus thing or another in order to deflate any amorous expectations he might have had. Sex became an unsafe place for him so he began masurbating. This was his only mode of sexual release for all those years.

"Layla, it's driving me insane," Madeline lamented. "He's perfect for me in every other way. But he can't maintain an erection during normal intercourse and a fulfilling sex life is very important to me. Do I break up with him over this?"

☞ Reeling & Dealing: This chapter on your Divorced Man's sexuality is located in the section "His Emotional Life" because sex *is* emotional for him. Of course it is physical too, but yours is a thinking man. Didn't you always want a man who thought less with his d**k and a little more with his head (the one set upon his shoulders)? Well, here he is. No matter where he is on the healing curve, assume that sex is a loaded issue for him, especially if he doesn't discuss it. The best remedy for the No-Dessert Option is time, coupled with a slow, yet approving approach. If you disparage him or

boss him around, he'll feel emasculated, and that defeats your very
purpose.

> *Though younger, Layla was surprisingly wise when it
> came to sexual brainteasers as we've already seen.
> "Why don't you go with it for now? If he wants to mas-
> turbate, then do it, but mutually. It's the most depend-
> able way of coming, and you can show him what you
> like. Besides, if you're crazy about him, you don't want
> to put pressure on him. These things generally have a
> way of working out over time."*
>
> *Madeline reported back several weeks later: Layla was
> right; her sex life was thriving. The lack of pressure, and
> the giddy fun of mutual auto-eroticism, ran its course
> and naturally turned into intercourse. It wasn't that
> Reg hadn't forgotten how to screw, he had just some-
> how lost the knack. Especially when it came to doing it
> with someone he had feelings for. Thanks to Madeline's
> ability to wait it out and to enjoy what they had
> together, it was back in full force. For Reg, it was just
> like riding a bicycle.*

Here is an example of a woman being able to handle sex in an
unafraid manner and find an inventive way to satisfy her lover without doing something she could not tolerate. Like a smart FateMate,
Madeline didn't take his love quirks personally. She cherished them
as a part of who he was. For Reg to be able to communicate his
sexual inadequacies to her meant that he trusted her. He wouldn't
or couldn't do that with just anyone.

While all FateMates may not be as adventurous and patient as

Madeline, the concept remains the same: Get him to relax sexually, then be creative, fun, and integrative with your approach so he can free himself of his past in order to establish intimacy with you. Always accentuate the positive aspects in your lovemaking. As long as you are not hurt or repulsed, why not play along with him? See how happy it makes him? You might enjoy it as well.

This process of opening up the No-Dessert Option man may take some time, maybe years. During this period do not forget that you deserve to receive pleasure too. It is paramount that he never stop trying to keep you sexually satisfied. If he doesn't, you will get frustrated, rightfully angry, and realize that he is selfish and not worth your compassion, energy, or the wait.

Lastly, as clichéd as it sounds, keep the romance alive. Whether your Divorced Man subscribes to the Smorgasbord or the No-Dessert Option plan, research shows that couples who view romance as a priority for the first two years of marriage are less likely to divorce than those who don't. And if that proves too difficult, there are always the wonders of Viagra.

PART III

HIS REALITIES

◈ 8. His Juggling Act ◈

It's bigger than the two of you.

EMBRACE COMPLEXITY

Between the X, his children, his job, a rapidly shrinking bank account that supports both his former and his current lives, and *you* all vying for his mind-share, the dynamics are complex. Your Divorced Man puts Ringling Bros. and Barnum & Bailey's three-ring circus to shame. Plus, once you are seriously committed to a Divorced Man, the FateMate family becomes an extended universe consisting of all the parents, grandparents, aunts, uncles, cousins, nieces, nephews, etc., from his first marriage, and now all of yours. Bigger does not necessarily mean better, but it does mean more complicated. Given the fact that his time is finite and precious, he can't possibly please everyone enough to satisfy their expectations, no matter how desperately he tries. He feels like a super-stretchy Gumby being pulled in every which direction.

☞ Reeling & Dealing: Entering into a relationship with a Divorced Man means taking on his commitments and priorities as your own. From here on in, learn to embrace his complexities. Seek to achieve what I call *heterostatis,* a balance of many seemingly conflicting things (*hetero,* meaning multiple + *stasis,* meaning equilibrium). Put in simple English, it can be a pain to deal with, but FateMates are multitaskers extraordinaire, so this should be a breeze for you. Hey, you always thrived on a good challenge—well, here it is.

Layla was thoroughly infatuated with her new flame, Bo. He was a venture capitalist whose work often took him overseas, while also fathering a son who lived with the X in a neighboring state. Even Bo's Palm Pilot was prone to crash because he had too much going on in too many places. Although Bo tried to spend all of his free time with her, Layla resented the fact that she was one of a string of things on his to-do list and not his first priority. Madeline helped her out. "Layla, if you really want to nab this one, you've got to get real. He's crazed with a zillion clashing stresses. If you can relieve him of some of his tensions, you're a champ. First, prioritize your own life. Then, if you can handle it, I repeat, if you can handle it, occasionally take his kid to a matinee, cook a dinner, pick up the laundry, or arrange the vacation. Volunteer to help with things you normally don't mind doing. The words 'Honey, let me help you' can go a long way. Yes, there is a certain degree of compromise and self-sacrifice involved, but making his life easier will make you indispensable. He will realize how much sweeter his life is with you in it and that he doesn't want to live without you."

And that's just what happened.

What you do not want to do is become a burden to him. If he does not perceive you as an asset, you will be earmarked for the liabilities column on his balance sheet. You must remember that his time with you means time away from everything else on his overloaded plate, so try to make those moments all the more special. Set your mind to making your time together extraordinary, so that he feels transported as he leaves his dutiful world behind. Complicated lives demand extra effort to instill passion.

Reciprocally, he must respect his time with you. While you need to remain somewhat flexible as he manages his numerous obligations, and even unanticipated ones like last-minute tutoring for his daughter's SAT exam the next day, he must be consistent and considerate of your time together as a couple. If he agrees to meet you somewhere at a certain hour, he needs to show you that he is trustworthy and dependable, just as you are with him, and just as he can be with his kids. Otherwise, you'll lose faith in his ability to commit to you.

Does this sound like a lot of work? It may be, but that's what comes from loving a Divorced Man. A lot more work, but hopefully a lot more rewards.

◈ 9. His X ◈

She's your X too.

The Anomaly

Rare is the FateMate who is blessed with an X she actually likes. In fact, it occurs with woefully so few FateMates that it's not worth my time or ink to write on this subject any further.

☞ Reeling & Dealing: Consider yourself lucky and enjoy!

The Archetypal Bitch

Don't delude yourself, his X inherently hates you. If he left her, I'm sure there's a good explanation, but suffice it to say that she's angry and rancorous. And if she kicked him out, she's still apt to be jealous and resentful as you usurp her reign of control over him. Menacing, maniacal, manipulative, she'll stop at nothing to make your new life together miserable. She wants her kids to hate you and will poison them with lies and malice to get her way. Her game is a zero-sum proposition: The more miserable her X-Husband is, the happier she becomes. This is especially true during the beginning stages of your relationship with your Divorced Man when she is more prone to panic as you begin to supersede his historic allegiance to her. Yet, no matter how depraved Xs may be, and you will read many X-cruciating examples in this chapter, our culture continues to treat the biological mother as a revered and sacred icon, while many Fate-Mates I know are better suited to mothering their Divorced Men's children than their real moms.

When you meet her, you'll likely ask yourself, "What the hell was he thinking? What could he have possibly seen in her?" Recall that wise old adage that all good men are losers at some point in their life. Chalk it up to the folly of his youth, with its impaired judgment, which we know is no longer the case since he desires you. As they say, timing is everything.

☞ Reeling & Dealing: A fundamental part of your FateMate's job is to make peace with *yourself* once you inherit an X. It is important to dig deep within and discover an inner strength that supports *compassionate tolerance* for her. Compassion in the Zen sense of having to continually remind yourself that all god's creatures on earth are beautiful and worthy of loving, including the (gulp) X; and tolerance in that you have no choice about her entering your life when you fall for a Divorced Man.

Once compassionate tolerance is achieved, based on my experience, the best advice is to minimize her presence in your life from the get-go. Delete any dreams of becoming best buddies. It almost never happens. So don't delude yourself into thinking you'll be the exception. After a while of trying to be her pal, the stab wounds in your back will scar, and you will finally understand that this notion is naive and idealistic. Rent the movie *Stepmom* and you'll see an absurdly unrealistic example of a loving relationship between a stepmother and a bio-mother plotline that only Hollywood could fabricate.

Resign yourself to simply cultivating a cordial relationship for those requisite family events when you must see her, such as at birthday parties, camp-visiting days, school occasions, and pickup/drop-off rendezvous between the X and your Divorced Man. *At his son's music recital, do you turn your hopefully blinding engagement ring into your palm or flash it boldly in her face?* Expect that a little *co-opetition* (cooperation + competition) on these occasions will be normal.

Maintaining your distance also gives you an air of superior remoteness, which means that the X has less opportunity to figure out your vulnerable points and therefore less occasion to manipulate you. Once your Divorced Man starts taking your advice as prescribed in *HTMADM* and stands up to her, she'll recognize your emblazoned influence on him and may even grow fearful of you. Once again I submit to you: The less she knows about you, the more power you hold.

Setting boundaries will also help you retain your sanity and your health. Never take on your Divorced Man's duties, such as scheduling weekends with the children, negotiating her divorce payments, or even the more mundane exchanges like arranging where to pick up the children. No good will come of it. This is your Divorced Man's responsibility. In fact, he should attempt to shield you from his daily tussles with the X, which will only rile you. In the beginning, if he feels the need to unload his own X files on you, lend an ear. But, if certain stories have no bearing on your life and only aggravate you, why listen? He should learn which stories to keep from you and which are fair game for sharing. In some cases, and this is one of the few times I will advise it, a little suppression on his part will do you some good.

X-Communicate

Curtailing unnecessary communications between your Divorced Man and his X is an important discipline for him to champion on his path toward a healthy separation. If he hasn't properly weaned himself from his past, he probably has itchy fingers that incessantly dial the X, often for no apparent reason, sometimes just to keep in touch. The contact relieves his internal unrest from an unwholesome addiction that is similar to one in which someone anxiously reaches for a cigarette, downs a cocktail, or sucks a thumb during disquieting moments.

And if he's not speed dialing her phone number, then rest assured, an ongoing deluge of phone calls will be headed in his direction from the X, especially if she hasn't remarried. She'll concoct frivolous excuses to stay in touch: The cat is stuck in the tree, the sink is clogged. You name it, I've heard it.

Or if she's subversive, she'll use her most powerful artillery, the children, and have them call to interrupt your life. They very well may have nothing to say, but no matter, the scheming X knows that when your Divorced Man hears their little voices she'll have succeeded in making him feel guilty over not being accessible to his children, and in injecting a somber note into his time with you.

> Layla was looking forward to her first vacation with Bo. She anticipated one sultry week of escapism in the Florida Keys, lounging in the sun and in their hotel room, with no work headaches, winter woes, or X interruptions. Or so she thought. With the "Do Not Disturb" sign firmly affixed to the doorknob, at seven A.M. on the first morning of their stay, they had a rude awakening. The X called in a tizzy, claiming she was ill, perhaps terminally so, and she needed to make arrangements for Gus to live with Bo in the event of her demise. She even prepped Gus. Oh, the heart-wrenching cries the little boy emitted through the phone! Later, when Layla asked Bo about the X's symptoms, he mentioned a

lump on her breast. "Could the X be jumping to con-clusions?" Layla asked herself. "But surely this had to be serious if she was involving her son."

Layla and Bo heard from the hysteric X at least twice a day, forecasting her doomsday scenario. Precious time together was consumed with talk of the X's tit. And when it wasn't, Bo was on the phone literally four hours a day, planning for Gus's transfer, setting up day care, schools, and the like.

When they returned from their so-called vacation, the X phoned, all chipper and spry. "I'll live!" she declared. "Am I supposed to jump for joy?" Layla pondered. The X's doctor had also just returned from his vacation and had diagnosed her lump as a premenstrual engorge-ment that would subside after her period. Layla and Bo had picked up the phone one too many times and naively fallen into the X's high drama. Never again, they swore to each other.

☞ Reeling & Dealing: If your Divorced Man doesn't do his share by restricting her intrusions into your lives, he is not innocent. By not redrawing the lines of communication, he may be enabling her manipulations and passively inspiring her deviant behavior. Subcon-sciously, he may even relish the sense of power he receives from her needing him, perhaps still loving him. Or he may get a thrill out of engaging in clandestine behavior with an X and a new FateMate both devoted to him. Or, maybe it's simply an old nasty habit. In any case, their relationship may then be considered co-dependent, which doesn't leave much room for you. Rest assured, the X will never move off her back and he'll never move onto yours within this framework. If he does not admit to this wayward behavior, suffice it to say that he doesn't grasp the strength of his tether to the X. If this situation rings true, he may get defensive and irate, and accuse you of being petty, insecure, or paranoid.

✐ TIPS: X-COMMUNICATING HER OUT OF YOUR LIVES

The following tips are helpful when X-communicating, or minimizing communications, with the X. Electronic and wireless technologies can be your best buddies, but only when you control them. Based on your Divorced Man's willingness, try to implement as many of the following guidelines as possible:

1. Under no circumstances is the X allowed to call you. If you live with your Divorced Man, the X's primary mode of communication should be with his cell phone. This gives you your privacy by eliminating any chance of your hearing her voice in the comfort of your own home. Have him inform her that home telephones are to be used for emergencies only when he is unreachable via cell.

2. Make sure your Divorced Man's cell phone is equipped with caller identification so he can see when she is calling him. If she goes the extra mile to block her telephone number from being defined on his cell phone's caller ID, presume that she is truly out to get him. In that case, your Divorced Man will have to exhibit self-control and refrain from answering the telephone when he sees the word Restricted *flashing on his cell phone screen. He will probably balk at this initially. After all, he'll argue, it could be someone else calling him who he needs to speak to. But have him try it for several days. Ah, how serene he'll find it. He'll then understand just how disruptive her calls are to his peace of mind and to your happiness together. And if he wants to please you, and keep you, then he will acquiesce.*

3. If she leaves a message on his cell phone, he should call her back only when it is convenient for him. *If no message is left, one can assume it's not important; therefore, no further action needs to be taken.*

4. Batch all contacts. *Your Divorced Man should gather several messages he needs to convey to her into one communication so that more frequent contact is not necessary. She should follow suit by his example. E-mail is a perfect medium for this.*

5. Turn off all phones before going to sleep. *Take particular care to be diligent about this during vacations when you want to spend more time cuddling in bed at any hour of the day or night. Take heed especially when your vacation takes you into a different time zone.*

6. During the workweek, have your Divorced Man confine the X's calls to his office during business hours. *We'll see how much he likes his meetings interrupted by her.*

7. Don't tell him what to say while he's on the phone with her. *That also means no passing of notes. Such unsolicited interference will only aggravate him and cause friction between the two of you. Your best bet is to smile and leave the room, holding your head high.*

One Divorced Man actually bought each of his three children telephones and paid their monthly bills so he could have direct access to them and avoid the X altogether. Eradicating the X from your life can be an expensive proposition, but the peace of mind purchased is priceless.

THE X FILES

Although to divorce legally means to sever the marital bond between a husband and wife, for some reason, Xs feel divorce gives them license to harass their former partners even more than when they were married. And while most FateMates secretly harbor vengeful X fantasies, it's the Xs who don't think twice about turning their revengeful visions into realities. If only she'd get over it and move on. She may not want him anymore, but she certainly doesn't want anyone else to have him either.

Here are a few pitiless X-antics that'll either: a) make you break into a cold sweat; b) gain a newfound respect for how ingeniously devious Xs can be; c) rejoice that in comparison, your X isn't that bad after all; d) happily furnish you with ideas for your next screenplay *Nightmare on Elm Street #6;* or e) laugh yourself silly.

WHAT FATEMATE DOES NOT HAVE AN X TALE TO TELL?

Just before her father and I walked down the aisle, I asked my stepdaughter, our flower girl, why she was wearing an old frock and not the gorgeous new dress that she and I had shopped for together. She didn't say a thing and just turned away. I later learned that her mother had returned everything we'd bought to the department store—for cash!

—Zena

I overheard my live-in fiancé arguing with his X on the telephone and of course I listened in. (Author's note: Obviously she hadn't read HTMADM.) I gleaned from his conversation that she'd broken her computer and had quickly laid claim to their daughter's new laptop, which was a Christmas gift from my fiancé. She warned Michael that if he didn't buy their daughter a new computer and deliver it that night, Trudy would not be able to hand in her book report the next morning and could potentially fail ninth-grade English. Before I could grab the phone out of his hand, Guilt-Ridden-over-the-Divorce-Michael capitulated. He purchased the laptop and delivered it immediately. Why can't he stand up to his X? And what will happen if we marry and share a bank account? Will my hard-earned dollars go toward his X's computer?!

—Jillian

When my boyfriend's son left for his first summer at sleep-away camp, his mother told us the bus left at nine A.M. when in fact it was really scheduled to leave at eight A.M. Her diabolical plan was to have us miss Max's big send-off entirely so he would think we didn't care enough to show up and she would emerge as the hero. Fortunately, we foiled her by calling the camp to double-check the departure time. I guess after all this time I've finally learned to anticipate her villainous ways.

—Suzy

The only positive part of all her meddlesome haranguing is that it reinforces for your Divorced Man why they are no longer together. And by default, you, or anyone, for that matter, come out looking like a saint.

☞ Reeling & Dealing: The truth is that, yes, in a sense, she is your competition—competing with you for precious resources such as his attention, time, and money. That said, as infuriatingly greedy as she may be, and as competitive as you may feel, try hard to remind yourself that you are not in a race with her. No one is keeping score. Therefore, it is not necessary to win. If you *do* imagine that you are in a contest with the X—*she lives a more comfortable life than he and I will ever be able to as a couple with the money she receives from my Divorced Man,* you will only ignite petty jealousies that will make you appear to be a nag, ultimately a very unattractive thing to your Divorced Man, and will probably remind him of his X anyway.

For the time being, let it go. Recognize that the one thing you *can* control is your reaction to her. Don't stoop to her conniving level, rise above it. Don't get riled up the way she wants you to. Why give her the satisfaction of letting her control any part of your life? Don't let her win. (*Oops!* I promised not to be competitive.) Isolate any outstanding envy that you may feel toward her and realize how much luckier you are—your man is no longer with her; he is with you now. The sweetest revenge is to be happy.

Using Herculean strength, resist the temptation to obsess about her. This means that you are to avoid thinking about her, talking about her, and bitching about her. Don't go there. X-tricate, X-tracize, X-orcise. Even refrain from eavesdropping when you hear her shrill voice shrieking through the phone pressed against your man's ear. Gracefully exit the room. Obsessive behavior is self-perpetuating and addictive. I guarantee that it will only make you depressed and/or disgusted.

Despite what your shrink may tell you, I'm all for bonding with your Divorced Man over disliking his X. Be on the same page; just don't overdo it. You and he really shouldn't need to have a common enemy to feel close to each other and she certainly doesn't deserve so much of your precious time and energy. In fact, she's probably not all that interesting. Instead, it's way easier to pity her. Any woman who delights in taking every opportunity to ruin your life clearly doesn't have one of her own. Now you're the one with an exciting new life to lead with your Divorced Man—so go live it!

Short of setting her up on blind dates, pray for divine intervention so that she finds happiness with another man. Only then will she be motivated to tone down her hostilities toward you, as she'll want to downplay her insanity to her new boyfriend, or shall we say *victim?*, and not present an X-Husband as a problem in her life.

Last, always remind yourself that time does heal. As you and your Divorced Man become closer, you will feel more secure in your relationship so that the anger she instigates will lose its intensity within you and will eventually slide off your back. Hard to believe, but I swear it's true. FateMates' word of honor. Also, with the passage of time, he will feel more beholden to you and therefore less so to her. Trust that with time and implemented wisdom from *HTMADM,* your happiness will become his main agenda.

Just a final note about the Good X, an oxymoron if I ever heard one. I know I said I wouldn't waste my time, but I don't want to be slipshod. Though rare, they do in fact occasionally exist. Remember, the Good X is not born—she is made by you. If you have the time, the patience, and the inclination, and if she's not genuinely evil, there can sometimes be a truce, mainly built around the children's well-being.

After all those years of marriage, Layla's mom was able to build a somewhat tenuous, but cordial, relationship with her current husband's X, primarily around the fact that they all loved to dance and would often meet at family affairs that had music. Layla's mom would graciously encourage her husband to dance with his X, who was so grateful, and still not remarried, that she mustered up the courage to speak to the woman who replaced her. At first, it was about the music, then it was the food, and then it became the children who they had in common. It didn't turn into a friendship, but when the X did remarry, Layla's mom and her stepfather were invited to the wedding. And they were thrilled to see that the new husband could cut a rug with the best of them. Yep, miracles can occasionally happen.

10. His Children

Don't forget: Your Divorced Man is also a daddy.

UNPLANNED PARENTHOOD

If you follow the advice in this book and all goes as planned with your Divorced Man, you are on your way to becoming an instantaneous parent. Now, just because you and your Divorced Man love each other that doesn't mean that you will be able to create an instant loving family with his children. It's generally a transition that's as easy as extracting blood from a stone, so set your expectations accordingly.

If they are of college age or older, you're basically home free as, legally, they're adults and hopefully act as such. If they're younger but decent kids, rejoice in your good fortune. If they're problematic, recognize that things were broken long before you entered the picture. If he doesn't have children, then you are truly blessed as the X will not likely be an ongoing intrusion throughout your otherwise idyllic life with your Divorced Man. However, bear in mind that over 65 percent of all FateMate relationships include children from his former marriage. Marriage may not be forever, but if he has children, divorce is.

☞ Reeling & Dealing: Put your perfectionist and martyr egos aside and don't dare dream of transforming yourself into the perfect stepmom. Yes, we all know that FateMates are superwomen, but face it, you will never replace their mother and, knowing what you know about her, why would you want to anyway? Besides, if you attempt to act as their parent, the kids will most likely shoot you down with a "You can't tell me what to do, you're not my mother" retort. This is why you are pursuing the path of a Fate*Mate*, not a step*mother*.

Instead, keep your FateMate participation with your Divorced Man's children light and festive. Rather than act as surrogates for their mothers, FateMates are best suited to being the cool new friend and role model. Ask yourself: How can I uniquely enhance the children's lives? By showing them a new and exciting world that the X does not, all the while maintaining your own individuality and interests, you create a win-win situation for all.

For instance, if they live with the X in the suburbs, do citified things that *you* (italics deliberately mine) and the children can enjoy, like visiting art galleries or off-off-Broadway shows. If the X lives in the city, then take the kids on nature expeditions. Your enthusiasm for the chosen activity will get through to them. Even if the kids complain, "It's weird!," which they are prone to do particularly between the ages of seven and sixteen, continue. In the long run it's good for them, and remember, we're thinking long term here. A happy kid today means a healthier one tomorrow. Think about the shrink's bills you can save by expanding their horizons now.

At an early stage in your romance, voicing criticism, displeasure, or passing judgment on his children or his parenting style is a no-no. Although it may be frustrating for a solutions-oriented FateMate like yourself to refrain from perfecting any imperfections you see, doing so will only ignite his fire and cause him to get defensive. Before you get proactively involved with the children's upbringing, I exhort you to wait until you move in together or until he asks for your opinion, whichever comes first.

Meeting the Kids

Once you're dating exclusively, the time may be right to meet the offspring of the man you adore. To win over your Divorced Man, you will need to have a positive impact on his children so that they give you the thumbs-up. Impressing your Divorced Man's kids is the latter-day equivalent of dazzling the parents of your high school prom date when *you* were a teenager. How times have changed.

> As in Layla's first meeting with Bo's son. After they survived their Florida vacation with the X's attempts to sabotage it, and once Layla proved herself indispensable to Bo, he went gaga over her and wanted her to meet Gus. Layla thought it might be hasty, but she was crazy about Bo. And after dating a string of losers, she decided she didn't want to dampen his enthusiasm. Together, they planned the perfect Saturday for the introduction: brunch at an outdoor café, rowboating in the park, and then a walk through the Egyptian wing at the Metropolitan Museum of Art.
>
> Gus was an adorable companion, excited, interested, and fun, much like his father. But being only eight, by the time they got to the museum, he was starting to get cranky and clingy, if not territorial, with Bo.
>
> Gus insisted that Bo carry him. And although Dr. Spock would argue that Gus was way past that stage of child development, Bo capitulated. Bo tried to put a good face on it, teasing him, trying to distract him, while trying to politely include Layla.

☞ Reeling & Dealing: If either you or your Divorced Man are not absolutely sure that this relationship has long-term potential or is sturdy enough to handle the introduction, delay meeting his tykes. Too many FateMates insist upon meeting the children too quickly, believing it will bring them more into their Divorced Man's life. What a mistake. Inserting his children into your love cocoon means inviting a host of highly charged emotional stresses, so why rush it? Instead of forcing the issue, relax and relish the time you have alone getting to know each other. There's no need to end this beautiful moment in your romantic history. The kids ain't goin' nowhere.

If you have trouble holding off, contemplate the scenario from the child's perspective by empathizing with the confluence of confused feelings he or she must be experiencing upon meeting you. Make sure you do the introductions way in advance of moving in together or getting married so that his children have time to adjust to you as the woman in their daddy's life, and as their new *Fate-Mother*.

Prior to the main event, find out if he typically introduces his kids to his dates to gauge how momentous an event this is for him and for them. Feel free to ask him how you will be introduced. As someone special? A girlfriend? A friend? This way he has time to think it through beforehand, while you can learn how he feels about you and how he chooses to present you to his immediate universe. Details such as these can be oh-so telling.

Just as many FateMates have firsthand knowledge of the importance of first impressions in the dating arena, initial introductions to his children can be the most lasting. On the day of your first meeting, have his kids spend some quality time with their dad alone so they get reacclimated to him, especially if they've been in the X's clutches for a period of time. Your Divorced Man should give them a preview of who they are about to meet. Then, it's time for your entrance. Ta da! If he has more than one child, consider meeting them separately. This will eliminate the dynamics of sibling rivalry, or their natural squabbling, and will allow you to get to know them as individuals. It is typically a calmer, pleasanter experience for everyone involved. And make no mistake about it, it's often a shock to many FateMate's systems to be around noisy, overbearing children. We're so accustomed to living on our own, for ourselves—is the word *compromise* even in our vocabulary?

Plan to get acquainted with his children in a casual setting for a friendly two-to four-hour stint. Map out an activity and environment that the children will surely enjoy. Some ideas, depending on their ages, are a casual lunch with an afternoon at a sports event, going roller-skating, or visiting an amusement park. Give them 100 percent of your attention without exuding overkill. Act just as you would when being introduced to a dear friend of a friend by keeping a considerate distance, all the while sustaining an engaged warmth. Move slowly at first, respectfully allowing the children to set the pace. They will draw you in when they are ready.

While in the children's presence, back off on setting out to claim your turf with your Divorced Man. If they need to cling to him at first, so be it. Let them sit next to him at dinner or hold his hand when you walk down the street. It is imperative that they understand that they still have their singular bond with their daddy and that you'll never take that away. Ideally, you don't want them feeling threatened. In fact, if anything, they should feel that you will enhance their experience as a family unit. Your prerequisite for enjoying a lifelong rapport with his children is to gain their trust from day one.

Instead of feeling like a flattened third wheel, Layla spoke up. "You know, I'm really beat. Perhaps we could stop for a while and have some ice cream in the museum's cafeteria. We can finish seeing the exhibit later. I also think there's a great book on ancient kings and mummies in the gift shop that we can pick up on the way to browse through while we're eating."

It was amazing how the combination of ice cream and a new book infused Gus with a sudden burst of energy. By the time they finished their snack, they decided to go home and rest, then see the remainder of the exhibit the next day. By reading Gus's mood correctly, and being tactful and giving, Layla became Gus's buddy in one fell swoop (or was that scoop?).

Many FateMates resort to showering the Divorced Man's children with gifts and, to a certain degree, this works. Other than on those special occasions when you do give gifts such as birthdays, holidays, graduations, etc., or when appropriate like when Layla purchased the book on Eygptian history for Gus at the museum, don't go overboard. In fact, I urge you to employ this strategy sparingly. After all, you don't want to condition them to believing that they'll be receiving presents on a regular basis or that you're bribing them for their affections. It will be a costly endeavor for you and not an honorable foundation for a relationship. Besides, their dad will typically be the one spoiling them.

Being true to yourself is always the best approach to earning their fondness. Have confidence that they'll grow to adore you for your winsome personality with or without extravagant enticements.

And if they don't, then you've got larger problems that even the lat-est Game Boy won't be able to fix.

As FateMates well know, age matters. Younger children are gen-erally more trusting and can adjust relatively quickly to an outsider; while adolescents, already in a hormone-driven frenzy, are prone to be more troublesome, often constituting a challenge to your wel-come. Though sometimes it seems as if you can't win, don't inter-pret any objections they may have to you as personal affronts. The kids are simply acting out in what can be an uncomfortable scenario. You're the adult, so keep the power by not letting their opinions rule you. FateMates should always approach meeting the children of their Divorced Man with an open mind.

How their dad treats you in front of them will indicate and drive how they deal with you. If there is the slightest doubt or waffling in his mind, they can sense it and will be protective of their dad and perhaps disrespectful of you. It is not permissible for him to bog you down with a laundry list of rules on what to say and not say or how to act when you are with his children. You need to be free to be you. The more relaxed and unified you are as a couple, the more the kids will revere the new union.

No doubt the X will expect a thorough debriefing from the kids upon their return from a first visit with you and your Divorced Man. The X will now know you exist in the flesh and surely milk them for details. How old are you? What were you wearing? What did you serve at each meal? Your hair color? Eyes? Do you have a weight problem? Any deformities to speak of? If they're of elementary school age, discretion is probably not their strongest suit. Instead, they may feel obliged to blab to their mother as she manipulates these relatively harmless creatures who are caught in the middle. This alone is ample reason not to argue with your Divorced Man in front of the kids, as the X is sure to hear all about it. Why give her the satisfaction? You and your Divorced Man can explain to the children the concept of honoring privacy, something they will appreciate as they enter their teens.

Knowing how important the children are to your Divorced Man, you'll want to continue fostering their father-child bond after you've met them. Allow them to see their daddy alone; this also gives you your own well-deserved downtime. Don't make them think you don't want to join them; rather, make it clear that you respect their need to have quality time alone with their dad. If anyone wants you, they know where to find you and you would be delighted to join them.

Last, before you commit to your Divorced Man forever, spend quality time, perhaps a vacation or two, with his children. If his children are truly problematic, you may opt to work it through, *or* bail out if you discover that their issues are insurmountable. Love can't always conquer the most obtrusive of inherited children, so you'll need to draw your own conclusions after giving it your best shot.

ALTERNATE-WEEKEND FATHERING

While the number of fathers singlehandedly raising their children has grown a whopping 62 percent over the past decade, to 2.2 million, over 90 percent of children of divorced parents still live with their mothers. That means that the Divorced Man is typically the noncustodial parent. His visitation rights can run the gamut, from daily involvement to no parental participation at all. Very often, the Divorced Man is an every-other-weekend father. Because this is a popular arrangement for Divorced Men, in this book we will refer to it as being the general rule.

Being relegated to the role of noncustodial parent, the Divorced

Man consequently plays a less significant role in rearing his children than he used to. Since he has only weekends with them, his time to make a real difference in their lives is limited; as a result, their compressed time together becomes ultraprecious and emotionally charged. He'll want to make it as pleasurable and action packed as possible to ensure that the kids will want to come back for more. This is why he's apt to refrain from disciplining them on their visits, thereby potentially turning your historically peaceful and fun-loving weekends into pure unadulterated and unadult havoc.

☞ Reeling & Dealing: Your Divorced Man may very well feel that he has little, if any, control over his children, as they will be more influenced by their live-in mother. This is especially frustrating for him if he doesn't like what he sees, such as unsightly table manners, unhygienic routines, or poor study habits. As his FateMate, you too may find it offensive when you see the X's genetic coding in their otherwise sweet faces, or the X's mannerisms habituated into their gestures. You may want to run in the opposite direction, but don't. Logistically, you or your Divorced Man can't stop the X's infiltration.

Your Divorced Man can choose to articulate his dissatisfaction to the X regarding her rearing capabilities, or incapabilities, as it were, but that could jeopardize how she treats him in the future. If she's truly malevolent, she can take it out on the children as an indirect, yet potent, way to punish him. For instance, limiting his access to the children is probably the most common way for Xs to assert their control. Then again, some Xs find other means of manipulation as they realize that X-Husbands are better and cheaper than baby-sitters or nannies.

If his children's well-being is at stake, it's up to your Divorced Man to consider whether or not to stand up to the X. In such cases, many Divorced Men will choose the path of least resistance with regard to the X if it benefits the child. He'll have to weigh this delicate trade-off with assistance from FateMate rationale, of course.

As difficult as it may be, he must eventually learn to accept the fact that if his children spend the majority of their time under their biological mom's spell, his relationship with them will change somewhat. Given his geographic limitations, he cannot possibly have the same impact on their lives. Accordingly, his expectations must be reduced and he must do the best he can under these revised circumstances. During the week, he may not be able to work on their homework in the family den, but he can purchase a copy of his son's biology textbook and study with him over the telephone. Or, he can even correct his son's homework via faxes or electronically delivered files. It's called *creative parenting*. And yet, no matter how much things may change for him in his postdivorce life, assure him that he will always be their father.

One of the most positive things that divorce can bring to children is an appreciation for different points of view. No longer are the children up against the united front of their bio-parents, so their father should be more apt to openly voice his views, which will often dissent from his X's. And vice versa. If the children live with the X, they may assume that her ways are the correct and only ways. With your refreshing FateMate outlook, you and your Divorced Man can give the children proper perspective. From these multiple standpoints, the kids can glean a sense of independent thinking. If your Divorced Man understands this, he will be comforted by your desire for his children's well-being and, consequently, will love and trust you more and sooner. When the raging hormones and the spirit of rebellion naturally induce his teenagers to become repulsed by everything their parents say and do, FateMates come out smelling all the sweeter.

Also, you must point out to him that as his children grow older, his relationship with them will naturally shift as they become more independent and pursue their own lives. Regardless of living with them or apart from them, as they age, he will lose a certain connectedness. This is an indication of a child's healthy maturation process, not to be mistaken as a sign that they no longer love him. Remind him of this when the time comes. The good news is that as he plays a lesser role in their lives, he'll soon comprehend that you're the one constant in his life. A terrific by-product and inadvertent consolation prize for you.

WHO'S CONTROLLING WHO?

When his overriding sense of guilt skews his concern for their well-being, meet the overindulgent dad. The blame he imposes on himself for the demise of his marriage propels him to act outlandishly and overcompensate for not being as integral a part of his children's lives as he once was.

> For Reg's daughter's fifteenth birthday party, she wants fifteen of her closest friends to sleep over in the tiny two-bedroom apartment Madeline (unofficially) shares with Reg for a weekend of Broadway shows, club dancing, and unrestrained shopping. Reg wants to start planning ASAP and insists that Madeline stay the weekend to help him supervise all those girls. Madeline adores Adele, but feels this request is over and above what she deems reasonable. Reg tries to convince her that all the teens do this and besides, it's his princess.

If you've never been privy to the kiddie party circuit, it can be a rude awakening. Each birthday party is painstakingly choreographed

to outshine the previous year's party as well as that of the neigh-
bors'. No one spends more lavishly than the Divorced Man. Their
fetes for their children can become increasingly elaborate, like the
one thrown by the divorced media executive who hired *Billboard*'s
hottest teen band to play at his child's thirteenth birthday bash.
Whatever will he do for next year's encore?

And, by the way, how's your stamina? Your time with the noncustodial Divorced Man is an exhausting succession of going from
one kid activity to another: wake up, feed kids breakfast, clean up
after them, hustle them to tennis lessons, shop for latest gadgets—
that the X is supposed to buy, mind you!—attend professional
sports game, consume junk food and mega-amounts of cavity-
causing candy, dine at raucous family-style restaurant—from the
day's constant motion there's not enough time or energy to cook at
home—see circus performance, then return home for dessert
number two, which contains a sugar content that keeps the prog-
eny bouncing off the walls all night. Tired yet?

God forbid your Divorced Man doesn't schedule every second
of the day or ever tell his kids to go and play, the way a nondivorced
father would. Racing from one activity to another, with no quality
hanging-out time to speak of, your Divorced Man may derive little
joy from the experience because he's so damn busy parenting, or
rather, doing what he *thinks* a good parent should do, schlepping
them from one activity to the next. Part of the fun of having children
is that you get to be playful with them. But not for this fella. Come
to think of it, that's why he needs you—to indulge him in his play-
time and bring out the little boy in him.

His extravagant gestures can be so out of control that even nondivorced parents are having their say. They're vehemently com-

plaining that divorced parents have raised the bar in terms of spoiling their children and that the nondivorced parents can't keep up. Can we have a sanity test here, please?

☞ Reeling & Dealing: The Divorced Man's regret over not being a larger part of his children's lives manifests itself in his boundless splurges on his children. Divorced Men need to understand that indulging in such excessiveness is not beneficial for their offspring. When you first explain this to him, he'll exclaim, "But my poor children. They're displaced, they're suffering." Suffering? *Pulleezzee!* Suffering is what you see in life-death scenarios, or in third world economies where there is little housing, medical, or educational services, malnourishment is rampant, a supportive family unit can be nonexistent, and survival is a day-to-day struggle. Compare that with the struggles of a child of divorced parents: two loving homes, two sets of clothes, two sets of toys, double the birthday gifts, etc. This hardly defines suffering.

You may be only dating now, but you need to start setting the tone of your relationship immediately. If you fail to do so, in one way or another, his excessive actions may be coming out of your hard-earned leisure time and paycheck. Temper his behavior now.

> *It takes all of Madeline's FateMate energy to quell her urge to rant and rave that Reg's daughter is spoiled. Instead, she wisely serves up a suggestion. Perhaps one evening of dinner and the theater for Adele's two best friends with a sleep-over saved for another occasion and a bigger apartment? This is an ideal compromise. Adele gets a special birthday bash, the promise of a treat to come, and understands that she can't always*

*get everything she asks for, while Reg no longer feels
that Madeline is an envious naysayer, but rather that
she is a team player willing to play ball. (Don't you hate
baseball metaphors?)*

*(When Reg wanted to further discuss a vacation with Madeline
and he said to her, "Let's parent this topic," she almost died laughing.
Since when was "parent" used as a verb to describe working though or
nurturing something other than children?)*

Even while you are engaging in fun activities with the children, you
may simultaneously feel an underlying jealousy toward them. It's
entirely normal. You'll wonder: Does he love them more than he
loves me? He should love them a lot—after all, you would want
him to be a doting dad for *your* kids together, wouldn't you?—but
he should also be excited by the prospect of restarting his life with
you. Feel free to remind him that these two priorities are not mutu-
ally exclusive. In his words and deeds, he should assure you that his
affection for his children does not diminish his love for you. Please
note that your competitive inclinations may feel somewhat similar to
those with his X, but unlike the X, these kids are blameless and
therefore do not deserve your wrath.

Consider this alternative: If he'd never had children, he might
not be as loving, committed, and unselfish as he is today. And if he is
a stingy father, run in the opposite direction. The FateMate mantra:
As the kids grow older and their lives become more independent, it
only gets easier for you. Countdown!

DADDY IS A MAN TOO

Divorced Men who were burned by their failed marriage sometimes become overly devoted fathers, at the cost of their manhood.

Such Divorced Men will overcompensate in their parenting as a subliminal substitute for true adult intimacy. Starting a new romance means opening oneself up to many unknowns and therefore the potential to be hurt again, while parenting is a role they know, feel comfortable with, and is something over which they can exercise a degree of control. To these men, parenting can become an obsession, at the expense of not allowing a FateMate to enter their lives and bring them testosterone-filled joy.

To the fresh-on-the-scene FateMate, it's exasperating to see these Divorced Men at the mercy of their children, catering to their every whim no matter how inane. *At the last minute he'll announce that his eleven-year-old daughter and her two girlfriends will be joining the two of you on your long-awaited romantic Saturday night out. Honestly, how many animated Disney films can a FateMate be expected to withstand?*

You're new to this, so you give him the benefit of the doubt and wonder if you're being exceedingly sensitive, or if he's just being a dedicated father. But what he's really doing is using the children as chaperones to buffer the romantic connection between you two. Chances are the only one with a happening sleep-over date this evening will be his daughter.

If his kids sense the clout they have with their father, they may experiment to see just how far they can go. For instance, they can elect to be a disruptive force between you and your Divorced Man by telling him that they don't like the new woman he's dating without giving him a reason. Or, more indirectly, they can impair your relationship by making it agonizing for him whenever you are around.

Early in Reg's relationship with Madeline, Reg made sure to plan enticing events for them with his two teenage daughters. But whenever he would do so, even if the girls were dying to go, they would protest vociferously and stage sit-ins where they wouldn't budge from their room. The message rang loud and clear: They weren't going to accompany daddy's new girlfriend, no matter how much fun the activity promised to be.

You're intact after arduous years at grad school; you've negotiated pay raises with the most ferocious of bosses; and here you find these sweet-faced tots pulling the marionette strings of your life. Is this some cruel twist of fate?

☞ Reeling & Dealing: Your Divorced Man must confront his fear of reentering a close man-woman relationship if he is to ever let you in and love again. First, you must help him understand that while he is a father, he is first and foremost a *man*. And as a man, he deserves to be loved by a woman. To deny receiving such pleasure, both physical and emotional, goes against biology (his Y chromosomes), and nature (the birds and the bees). You may want to revisit Chapter 6's "Tips: Rebuilding His Self-Esteem" to rearouse his masculine disposition, which may have been repressed or dormant for some time.

In any case, once again, don't ever take it personally. It has everything to do with your Divorced Man's relationship with his children and little to do with you. The kids are acting out, reigning sovereign over their domain. And who could blame them? It's a scary prospect from their point of view. They don't like the idea of a new woman prancing into their lives, stealing their daddy's affection; replacing their mother; or if your Divorced Man has an objecting teenage girl, usurping her role as the woman of the house. *Knowing this, however, did not help Madeline get past her feeling of rejection.*

In order for your Divorced Man to reconcile himself to the fact that he can be a loving father and a loving man in a relationship with a FateMate, it'll help to have him understand the genesis of his children's power play, as stated above. It's up to him to have frank discussions with his children to assure them that their best interests are foremost and set their minds at rest. Ultimately, he can explain to them that they want their daddy to be happy as a man and as a father. In fact, a happy man makes a happier father.

For the candidate FateMate, tread gingerly in the background, until you get the green light to enter the family picture. Causing rifts between him and his children at an early stage in the relationship is a mistake. With his allegiance to his children much stronger than the one he has to you, most likely you will be the one to be escorted out the door.

> To his credit, Reg explained to Madeline that this was between him and his girls as he attempted to have heart-to-hearts with them, but to no avail. They wanted their daddy for themselves. Reg explained to Madeline that he felt powerless and under their control and didn't feel comfortable causing further problems in his home. It was evident that he wasn't yet ready to assert himself as a man with needs and go against his daughters' wishes. When Madeline sensed that he was on the verge of giving in to the stubborn duo, and she was soon to be given the boot, she took matters into her own hands.
>
> Madeline had noticed that Reg's teenagers cast a resentful and jealous eye over her alluring wardrobe,

makeup, and jewelry. Madeline was entitled to the fruits of her labors, but obviously Iona and Adele didn't seem to think so. So, being the clever FateMate, she decided to confront the issue head-on. "If you can't beat 'em, join 'em. After all, I had nothing to lose," she reasoned to herself.

So, the next time the girls slept over, she happily displayed her things, letting them try on whatever they wanted, all the while complimenting them on how adorable they looked. Making up their faces, teaching them new hair tricks, playing dress-up with the girls, this was an area in which their mother had no talent or inclination (although she was an expert in denigrating Madeline's flair any chance she got). It became the thing that the girls most looked forward to on their every other weekend with their dad, and soon Madeline was also enjoying herself tremendously. And of course Reg was delighted with the fashion show his three favorite girls put on for him.

Because of Madeline's ingenuity, she was no longer perceived as a threat to the status quo of Reg's relationship with his children; instead, she became a welcome addition, providing him with the love he deserved and the support he needed in raising his daughters.

◈ 11. Money ◈

Money may not be an issue while he's wining and dining you as a prospective girlfriend, but when you become a serious FateMate, that's when the cabernet sours and the soufflé collapses.

THE GREAT DRAIN

The reality is as unromantic as it gets. Money is finite—whatever amount he gives them, it is that much less for the two of you. Some refer to it as *economic polygamy*. In most cases, the X receives the house, plus a monthly stipend from your Divorced Man that covers alimony and/or child support. To make matters worse, this monthly check often does not include the children's peripheral expenses he may also be bound to absorb: tutoring, extracurricular activities like tennis lessons, camp, private school, medical attention, vacations, and *ouch*, four years of college. "You give her how many f***ing dollars per month?" It's a bottom-line proposition.

And while you know that money is literally a commodity, merely a slip of paper, on a personal level it takes on a very deep significance for you. It becomes a metaphor for all things dear: your love, security, freedom, empowerment, and future. In fact, it is a major hot button for most people: 57 percent of divorces are about money. Let's not become part of this statistic, shall we?

Now, can we talk? As a self-motivated FateMate, you are financially independent, bringing your own assets and earnings to the relationship. And even though you are not seeking a man for financial security, let's be perfectly frank, you always dreamed that together, your household income and lifestyle would be greater than if you lived as a single woman. With a Divorced Man, t'ain't necessarily so.

☞ Reeling & Dealing: It'll take you a while to fully comprehend the humongous impact of his spousal and child-support payments on your life. Like any significant loss such as a death, a stock market recession, etc., you'll undergo a progression of emotional stages in order to deal with his financial reality, which has now become yours. The first phase is denial: "I love him, it doesn't matter that his X lives in a mansion, while we live in a tenement." Following, is anger: "Because of that bitch, we can't afford to go to Hawaii this year. When did you say the support payments end?" Then comes regret: "I wish I had never fallen in love with him. Woe is me." And last, the resolve: "We'll make this work. What is important is that we love each other and are committed to a future together." Be fore-warned, this cycle could last for years.

We all agree, money is a painfully sensitive topic to broach, but you'll need to understand his financial commitments to the X and children before you finally commit to him. Will he let you read his divorce agreement—certainly not as thrilling as the latest best-seller—so that you have a crystal-clear understanding of his mone-tary obligations for the near and long term?

Look forward to an ongoing negotiation for the rest of your lives together, so start practicing immediately and get proficient at it. Avoiding these issues in the beginning will haunt and possibly harm you in the future. As onerous as it may be, try to plow through this necessary discomfort with a smile.

Hey, What About Us?

Once you enter an exclusive relationship, you will most likely experience overwhelming resentment when you see a large chunk of his paycheck allocated to the X. Similarly, you'll hyperventilate when you witness him paying out-of-pocket expenses for his kids that are above and beyond his divorce-decreed financial obligations.

> One Saturday afternoon, Layla and Bo planned to pick up Gus at the train station and whisk him off to a sun-filled day at the beach. But when Gus arrived, he declared a different agenda. In his little hand, he held a wish list—mind you—written in adult script of items to be purchased that day: a train set, two schoolbooks, a hockey stick, and the latest Sony PlayStation. Layla could not believe what she was witnessing—nor could I when she showed me the list. Even though it was the X's responsibility to provide Gus with these items from the generous child support Bo gave her, evidently the X had murmured to Gus a "Go ask your father."
>
> Layla's yoga deep-breathing exercises came in handy. "Now is not the time to discuss this," she seethed, "however, if you and I ever become serious, this will have to stop." So, instead of the glorious afternoon Layla had anticipated, the day turned into a shop-till-you-drop marathon—and we're not talking Neiman Marcus.

Meditate on that Zen of inequity. The X inserts the child in the middle of her money power play knowing full well that Bo will gladly pay so as not to disappoint Gus or come off as the bad guy. When tallied, these shopping sprees can burn a larger hole in your Divorced Man's already charred pocket.

☞ Reeling & Dealing: If you feel it may be too early in your relationship to be having money conversations, you can voice your concern as a potential problem that might have to be addressed down the road. Until you feel comfortable enough in the relationship to correct his out-of-control splurging, you will find that sometimes it helps to shield yourself from it, simply don't accompany them to the toy store. Out of sight, out of mind. Ignorance is bliss. For the time being, excuse yourself, citing you have work to complete at the office, an eyebrow wax, or a lunch with a friend, whatever works for you, I'm all for it. Allow me to repeat: This is a temporary remedy during the earlier stages of your love.

Your resentment will surely escalate if your lifestyle is adversely affected. *Why do the children get the new PlayStation and I end up cooking instead of going out to dinner?* His divorce may have left him financially strapped, but when it comes to his children, he still spends as if he's King Midas. Help him distinguish between his obligations to his family and his remorseful feelings for not being there for them 100 percent of the time physically and emotionally. Explain to him how he tends to act out this internal conflict through money, which may be temptingly easy for him, but ultimately is not a healthy message to convey to his children. If the kids' requests get out of hand, their father must sit them down and clarify that daddy pays mommy sufficiently and that they are to ask mommy for money to cover their everyday needs. Even kids from nondivorced households learn how to negotiate with parents for what they need or want. It's part of growing up. Don't let him deny his children this rite of passage.

In any case, if the guilt continues to ooze out of his pores and he can't help but pour out extraneous expenditures on his children, you must rein in his obsessive behavior. When this occurs, I know it's almost impossible not to want to reach for a heavy object with which to wound, and I absolutely agree with you that he deserves to be the brunt of all your fury, but for the sake of your own sanity, try to deal with this rationally.

> Several months later and deeper in love, Layla indirectly proposed an idea to Bo. She nonchalantly mentioned her friend Dean, who had a similar predicament with his X. Every other weekend, Dean's daughter would return to her primary residence, where she lived with her mom, with the items purchased by Dean for her that weekend. One day, Dean decided that these items should be considered part of the X's household since his daughter was using them at home, and therefore the X's expense. Consequently, he started deducting these expenses from her next month's support check. Dean's X was furious. "How dare you penalize me for your own inability to curb in your neurotic spending on your daughter?" As loath as Dean was to admit it, she was right. That sent a long overdue jolt to his credit-card-swiping habit.

> After a couple of months of back and forth, Dean and his X jointly came up with a solution. They agreed to agree in advance on the must-have items Dean would buy his daughter, which could be subtracted from his support payments to his X. This was a win-win compromise: His X delegated him to shop for goods where he

*had a particular proficiency, such as electronic equip-
ment, thus saving the X time and effort. Plus, Dean
still looked like a hero in his daughter's eyes and was
able to satisfy his uncontrollable itch to shop for her,
though he tempered it somewhat.*

*Moreover, Dean's girlfriend came to the rescue. Apply-
ing her creative FateMate juices, she composed a list
of enticing activities for them to share with Dean's
daughter on her weekend visits so that shopping no
longer was an afternoon's destination in itself. This
FateMate rationale was right on target—let his daughter shop with her girlfriends at the local mall, while they
showed her fun in other less consumer-driven ways.*

*Dean kept absolutely accurate records and diligently
sent copies of the receipts to the X so that every item
was accounted for.*

This reminds me of one Divorced Man who was so guilt ridden that
he'd faithfully cut a check to the X after she simply told him the
month's sum of extraneous expenses that she claimed he was to
pay for. This dollar amount included the kids' tutoring, medical, and
camp, as well as the X's own padding. He never requested receipts,
canceled checks, or an itemization of her outlays. No wonder she
was driving around in a spanking-new car with a skinny new nose.
The lesson: Xs are also to submit records of receipts for all items
before any reimbursement occurs.

   On the exceptional occasion when these X-tra payments do
not negatively impact you and there's more than enough money to
go around, you still may experience an irrational sense of depriva-

tion. Chapter 13, "Your Emotional Legacy," addresses this in more detail, helping you uncover and rid yourself of this anxiety.

SELF-PROTECTION

Most important, after working hard your whole adult life and earning your own assets, financial self-protection is critical. This means conserving and growing what you brought into the relationship as well as investing in your future as a couple.

> Madeline had always dreamed of going back to school for a Ph.D. in art history. For years, she had been setting aside money toward this end and finally had saved the complete tuition; but because she loved her job and quite frankly needed her income to support her high-end city lifestyle, she delayed her academic pursuits. However, as she grew closer to Reg, she began to envision a life with him in which she could eventually leave work and devote herself to her studies, enabling her to embark on a new career as an art professor (and perhaps as a wife and mother?).
>
> As she and Reg talked about commingling their finances, she was very clear about the money she had designated toward her studies. She explained to Reg that as an independent woman, she did not want to ask "permission" to pursue her dream. Therefore, she planned to keep this money in a separate account, earmarked for her studies.

The good news about marrying at a later age means that, typically, both your current careers and status in society are better indicators of your long-term socioeconomic potential than they were earlier in your lives when you and your Divorced Man were starting out in the world. Therefore, when you eventually take the plunge and intertwine your finances, you will have a better sense of your respective financial futures and can plan accordingly. And the old maxim is true: Two heads are better than one. It is a fact that married couples manage money more adroitly. Plus, research has shown us that married women have a higher earning potential primarily due to a spouse's encouraging guidance and a marriage's support system.

☞ Reeling & Dealing: Ultimately, it is a question of what is most important to whom, and how compromise can be reached without either partner feeling compromised.

> Reg was a fair-minded man who understood that he alone was responsible for his child-support and alimony payments. He was happy to support Madeline's aspirations, and saw no problem with her separate account. They agreed that they'd watch their expenses and hunker down as necessary until her schooling was over and she was earning a salary once again.

In an ideal circumstance, your Divorced Man has a separate bank account that has enough funds in it to subsidize the financial commitments of his first marriage on an ongoing basis. In this way, his mandatory monthly withdrawals for the X do not adversely affect your joint savings or lifestyle together. Unfortunately, most Divorced Men do not have enough money to accomplish this after being financially strapped from the divorce. If your man is not in as good a financial position as Reg, or resents your keeping a separate account, you may want to have open discussions about what this means to you, how important it is to your future happiness, and either he appreciates your position or you must consider that your nest egg may someday go toward his kids' orthodonture work.

As a FateMate envisioning a future with a Divorced Man, I suggest you consider maintaining your own income. Not only will you most likely need the extra revenue, but if your Divorced Man is the designated breadwinner, the balance of the relationship may shift out of your favor. It's simply harder to function as equals when one partner controls the flow of money. Think of it as akin to an adolescent asking her dad for money to go to the movies. It's okay for a high-schooler, but not the healthiest route to take as an adult. If you decide together that you will be the one to forfeit earning power, for instance, to help raise a family or to travel with your husband, this could entail a redefinition of your identity and it could take time for you to make the transition. Most overachieving FateMates are not accustomed to being dependent on a man. With your dignity intact, make sure you are protected and have what you need going forward, no matter what amount you require.

Once you've established the trust of your Divorced Man and are securely in a committed relationship, you may want to consider managing, or participating in the management of, your finances as a couple. The knowledge you gain will make you feel in control, alleviating any uncertainties in your mind where doomsday scenarios and distrust typically breed. If this is not an area of expertise for you, educate yourself so that it becomes one. Start by setting up a file system and being responsible for opening and organizing the mail. Later, graduate to paying bills. For example, is the X's AOL account still automatically showing up on his monthly credit card bills? If you discover that it is, now you can call it to his attention and fix it immediately.

You may want to volunteer to manage a monthly accounting of

your expenses together as a couple. Create a budget that reflects his prior obligations from his first marriage, any you may have, your lifestyle needs such as travel, entertainment, etc., and your future long-term goals as a partnership (a family of your own, education, housing, etc.). Are you able to save a prescribed amount of money each month to meet these goals? How much is flowing in and out? This will surely take time and effort, and will probably put you in a lousy mood. But someone's gotta do it and you'll feel more empowered if it's you.

✐ **TIPS:** THE FINANCIAL PROS
Enlisting the assistance of a professional could help you get on securer ground.

1. A Certified Public Accountant
In most cases, you'll be looking for a CPA with practical experience in divorce matters. In particular, find someone with good analytic skills and a background in investigative accounting so that like a clever sleuth, they'll be able to ferret out, if necessary, the details behind the face value of his X's statements. You'll also want your CPA to have a keen understanding of taxes and their implications as it relates to you and your filings with the beloved IRS.

For example, the first couple of years of marriage to your Divorced Man is when the X's revenge tactics are most inspired. If she's a money-grubbing X, an accountant might advise you to keep your funds in separate accounts and to file your taxes separately from your Divorced Man. Just in case the X gets off on subpoenaing your Divorced Man, your personal finances will not be subject to scrutiny and, therefore, not revealed in a court of law. You might end up paying higher taxes, but the peace of mind is inestimable. Later, when the coast is clear, go ahead and establish a joint bank account. It takes a certain amount of trust to intermingle funds, but if you can't trust your Divorced Man, then hey, why are you with him?

2. A Certified Financial Planner

If you have, as they say, high-class problems—and one can only hope that this is the case—a CFP can help define financial goals and offer a broad range of financial-planning options. He or she will assist you in adjusting to a new income lifestyle as you start your life with your Divorced Man. Similarly, your CFP can aid you in regard to postdivorce taxes, money and risk management, life insurance policies, and retirement planning. The planner can work with your accountant and attorney to help collect, organize, and analyze financial data, calculating your short- and long-term needs as a couple.

Overall, the CFP's job is to help you develop a personalized strategy to gain control of your financial future. You may not think that your assets warrant this, but what you have now may be tapped and zapped if you don't seek to maximize it. It's also a great way to find out what your Divorced Man has and how sharing he tends to be. A FateMate decree: As your love and trust grow, so too should his generosity.

In order to find a CPA or CFP who works best for you, interview several candidates. Gather at least two references per each engagement and contact them to learn how others gauged their competency. Obtaining recommendations from a divorce attorney who is well respected in your community is a good start (see the next chapter, "Legalities"). Your lawyer may have to work closely with both experts, so give him or her the opportunity to furnish you with his or her preferences. Always check credentials, education, experience, and fee structure upfront. Select the one who is best qualified to suit your needs and whose personality best meshes with yours and your Divorced Man's. I hope it never comes to this, but just to be safe, be sure to ask if he or she has a lot of experience testifying in court and is knowledgeable about the judicial system in your locale.

12. Legalities

Just when you thought the "courtship" phase
of your relationship with your Divorced Man was over . . .
his X redefines the term for you.

YOUR SENSE OF FAIRNESS

Whoever wrote "all's fair in love and war" was probably an X.

> *Right after the divorce, Reg's X quit her job since, with*
> *the help of her cutthroat divorce lawyer, she was able*
> *to comfortably live off the child-support payments Reg*
> *was paying. Gas, phone, water, mortgage, gardeners,*
> *food, taxes, you name it—Reg kept his children and his*
> *X in the lifestyle they were accustomed to. When the*
> *X recently remarried, her new husband moved into the*
> *very house Reg pays for. In effect, Reg was paying for*
> *his X and her new husband's room and board.*

So why doesn't the X's new hubby just ask Reg for an allowance?

☞ Reeling & Dealing: The sooner you come to terms with the fact that divorced life is not fair, the better off you will be with your Divorced Man. The injustices will abound, and you are bound to be a victim of injustices. Unfortunately, that's just the way it goes. It will be painfully frustrating for an intelligent and persistent FateMate like you to remain passive when confronting such inequities. After numerous bouts of "It's not fair!" and scheming to right such glaring wrongs, you will eventually understand that your efforts are often futile. You will have to consciously stop yourself from intervening because, in some cases when you do, you can do more harm than good.

In the above scenario, if Reg chose to take his X to court to reduce his payments to her, a court could easily rule in favor of Reg's X simply because that was what the original divorce agreement stipulated and because courts tend to be partial to the X anyway. Backfire! An unsympathetic judge, who might be an X herself masquerading as an objective court official, could determine that Reg should not only subsidize his X's second marriage but also mandate that he pay his X an additional monthly fee that would end up supporting their new baby. It happens.

> *Together, Madeline and Reg determined that to start legal action might cost them more money and aggravation in the long run, so they opted not to protest and to continue funding his X's new marriage under the guise of "child-support" payments. Desperate to look at a bright side, Madeline and Reg declared that they were just thankful that the X duped someone into marrying her so that she could now redirect the attention, which had been fixated on them, to her new husband. Better him than them.*

Ever dream you'd watch TV reruns of *Divorce Court* for solace?

LITIGIOUS LOGISTICS

Many FateMates have Xs who thrive on taking their X-Husbands, or threatening to take them, to court. When Xs initiate court battles, they typically want more money or control. Ironically, it is often the Xs who are subsidized the most generously by their former husbands who can afford both the time and money to retain a lawyer for filing lawsuits that only serve to plague their X-Husbands and you. Sometimes, she will become aggressive simply because she can. Or sometimes she has nothing better to do. Other times, joyous life events for you and your Divorced Man will prompt her wrath. Specifically, landmark occasions such as her first recognizing your existence in her X-Husband's life, your moving in together, your getting married, and your having a baby, will arouse the killjoy spirit in her.

☞ Reeling & Dealing: If after reading *HTMADM* you are happily planning to marry your Divorced Man (please E-mail me so I can congratulate you!), I thoroughly recommend meeting with a legal expert who can help you lay down a durable foundation for your new life together.

Although you might not need one now, if you have a litigious X, it's a smart idea to have a divorce attorney familiar with your Divorced Man's agreement in your arsenal of experts should you require—and I hope you don't—his or her services. Your prevention can be the key to squelching her intervening. Maybe you'll opt to retain him or her for your prenuptial or postnuptial agreement too, should you elect to have one or the other—then be sure to ask for a two-for-one discount.

To start, together with your Divorced Man, sit down with the attorney he used for his divorce, that is assuming your Divorced Man thought this professional did an excellent job. During this meeting, assess whether or not he or she is up to snuff for any legal issues you may encounter down the road. Be prepared, the conversation is not apt to be a pleasant one as you'll learn how your

Divorced Man, who normally can be so savvy in areas of business, was such a dope when he negotiated with his X. Or you'll discover that he's fixated on bequeathing his entire estate to his children from his first marriage—a foolproof sign of a man stuck in the past—run, do not walk. In any case, your Divorced Man's mind set should be clearer and more concerned with building a future than when he originally retained the lawyer for his divorce. If this lawyer does not possess the necessary qualifications, proceed to find another.

Selecting a lawyer is an important decision that should be done carefully. Make sure you can find one you can trust, who matches your philosophy, and one with whom you feel comfortable spending time. He or she must know the law, possess honed negotiating skills, be familiar with the key players in your local judicial system, and have extensive experience practicing divorce and family law.

✐ **TIPS:** QUESTIONS TO ASK A PROSPECTIVE DIVORCE LAWYER

Here is a list of basic questions to refer to when interviewing a candidate attorney with your Divorced Man. Customize this list, adding or deleting questions, based on your Divorced Man's divorce particulars. Prepare to provide full disclosure pertaining to all issues so that the lawyer can offer you his or her best possible response.

1. Do you practice divorce and family law exclusively? If not, what percentage of your business is attributable to these areas?

2. How long have you been practicing?

3. What is your retainer? Is this fee deducted from future costs? What is your hourly rate? How often will you bill?

4. What percentage of your cases go to trial? Are you willing to go to trial?

5. Can you comment on my Divorced Man's divorce agreement? Do you see any red flags we should be aware of? How can we protect ourselves in the near and long term?

6. If the X has hired an attorney and a particular case is in the works, how much do you estimate it will cost? How long do you estimate it will take? What are our odds of winning this case?

7. Can you please provide us with two client references who have situations similar to this?

Based on his more personal experience, your Divorced Man can also offer alternative outcomes from a multitude of perspectives as you weigh the trade-offs in deciding whether or not to pursue legal action. How will his children be affected? Will it place undue strain on his relationship with the X? His X's relationship with the kids? And his relationship with toi? There is often more at stake than meets the eye. So, before you insist on skipping down the righteous path, you'll need to stop yourself and ask, would you rather be right or loved?

PART IV

YOUR
DECISIONS

◈ 13. Your Emotional Legacy ◈

In this section, we examine what you, Dear Reader, bring to the relationship. We temporarily cease dissing the usual suspects—which is infinitely easier and a helluva lot more fun—and admit that we FateMates have our own baggage (more like handbags, less like luggage) when it comes to our relationships.

YOUR FEARS & ANXIETIES

Net-net, what's really at stake are the three *i*'s: *intimacy, investment,* and an *infant*—and if you will get them. Due to his responsibilities from his prior marriage, his time, energy, money, and even his ability to love may be constrained. Can you deal with not getting 100 percent of him? With sharing him? With extensive compromise? With potentially not getting what you want—a weekend of undivided attention, a life-insurance policy, or a child—because he had a past with someone you wish never existed?

For many FateMates, his divided loyalties stir up powerful feelings from the past. What psychological predisposition do you have and how does it influence your relationship with your Divorced Man? For instance, if you didn't get enough love from your parents or have experienced sibling rivalry, his real-life limitations may evoke the feeling that you'll never get enough of him, leaving you to feel slightly slighted. Or, if you are a product of divorced parents yourself, perhaps you are prone to fears of abandonment. Subliminally, you may even be looking for a daddy replacement. As a result, his restrictions could reawaken within you deep impressions of betrayal. To compound this, you may possess the far-flung fantasy that Prince Charming will sweep you off your feet, rescue you from singledom, and ride with you into the sunset. Are such delusions impeding or advancing your relationship?

☞ Reeling & Dealing: There's nothing worse than feeling unfulfilled, unprotected, or unloved—especially while you have a steady lover. How to eliminate such agonies? First, do your analytic homework. Focus your competitive, perfectionist, I-want-it-yesterday personality into seeking control over what you can affect: *yourself*. Your primary job is to isolate the disturbing sensations being aroused within you, explore their origins, and learn how to repair them so that they don't impair your love. Cut to the core and ask yourself, are my anxieties being driven by my Divorced Man's situation or are emotional hang-ups from my unresolved issues being exacerbated by my Divorced Man's situation? Invoke the help of a psychological expert if necessary.

> *So what's up with Layla? After Bo returned from a camping weekend with his son, he hinted to her of the possibility of a monogamous, live-in relationship. Instead of flying straight to heaven, Layla panicked. She initiated an absurd argument over not being consulted on selecting the color of his new car (like she really gives a damn, right?) and didn't return his calls for three days.*

> *When she told Madeline what had happened, Madeline couldn't help herself. "Are you insane?" she said. "Okay, so he has relics of a former life that still live and*

breathe with him, but who hasn't? The point is that he's an incredible catch. You should be ecstatic." Layla cowered, then incoherently mumbled something about not having his full commitment. But deep down she knew she wasn't being honest with herself.

As much as Layla desperately yearned for a man, she was terrified of having one in her life. With the help of an insightful shrink, she was able to examine this conflicting duality. Layla finally understood that the turmoil existed within herself. Since she was the product of parents who had divorced bitterly and had a father who had denied her the attention she had craved as a child, it's no wonder she had been dating so frenetically. The underlying message of her parents' divorce was to not trust the institution of marriage, that it is destined to fail, and that she would be left alone just as she was as a youngster, or just like her mother was. Hence, her noncommittal flights of dating fancy and a history of picking unavailable men. Bo's divorce issues intensified her deep-seated fears.

Like many FateMates, Layla was accustomed to serial relationships, beginning with hope then ending in disappointment, over and over again. Eventually, the pattern became self-perpetuating, where she would break off the relationship before her lover did. Layla thought that it was better to be the leaver instead of the leavee— that there was less hurt this way. And with a Divorced Man, the propensity for a FateMate to skip out when the going gets tough is even more compelling. It's all too easy to rationalize, "I don't need this. I can return to my former free-spirited self instead of feeling burdened by the weight of his problems due to his past mistakes." With logic like this, Layla avoided the risk of being abandoned by a man, but she also avoided the bliss of a committed relationship.

If you're like Layla (or like me, for that matter), a FateMate with a control-freak streak, you will immediately try to modify situations in order to squash any anxieties that make you feel rejected. You may pout and withhold love until he shows you that he is willing to give up his past for you. You may think that if he sacrifices a prior obligation to his X or children, then he truly cherishes you. But this strategy is flawed. You're mistaken to think he'll love you more by making him skip his daughter's soccer game. And the reality is that if he did, he'd be mopey all day, with his resentment stewing and this would eventually attack your relationship in one way or another. So, with all this in mind, sweetly and graciously let him go about his duties so that he doesn't resent you for having missed his child's music recital. I assure you that when he returns from the outing, he'll be all the more adoring.

Coping with his split loyalties means accepting his reality and making the most of the situation. A FateMate must avoid the temptation to view his time away from you as his leaving you all alone. He is not abandoning you. Instead, relish the freedom. Use this as an opportunity to enhance your life. Take a yoga class like Madeline and Layla, start a book club, or go scale Mexican ruins. Console yourself with the fact that he's dutifully fathering instead of wasting time and money on an unsavory addiction such as chronic gambling or chatting with strangers on the Internet. Remember that he had a life before meeting you, just as you did, and much of that experience is what makes him so special to you. A rule of thumb to keep in mind when the going gets tough for you: If he's good to his kids, he'll be good to your children together.

If Layla wanted this Divorced Man, she'd have to undergo further soul-searching and combat her anxi-

eties, two of her least favorite pastimes. After much introspection, she defiantly decided, "I refuse to let my fears hijack my emotions and get the better of me. I'll never find true love without feeling vulnerable. Bo is worth the effort." Layla called Bo back, explaining her inner revelations, and enrolled in a pottery class during Bo's Saturday mornings with Gus. Bo was a perfect gentleman about it, hanging in there, accepting her for who she was. We like him all the more for it, and so does Layla. In fact, she's composing her move-in-with-Bo to-do list as I write this sentence.

Although your Divorced Man may be a daddy, you should not look to him to be yours. Yes, you can see that he's paternal and nurturing by the way he treats his children, but if loving a father figure is your idea of a romantic relationship, a Divorced Man may not be the healthy choice for you. Do you really want to play the role of the child and then find yourself in competition with his children? I don't think so. Furthermore, you wouldn't be able to successfully Fate-Mother his kids when the time comes. His sobering realities are for adults only. Being a FateMate means participating in a partnership of equals.

Another self-defeating syndrome standing in the way of your happiness with your Divorced Man is idealizing how your relationship *should* be. From a girlish age, you've probably savored the fantasy that you are a princess (don't let anyone tell you otherwise), and that he will be a white knight in a shiny new Mercedes, with drop-dead looks, the bankroll of a Rockefeller, the *savoir faire* of James Bond, and someone your mom would approve of. Though I agree that you are entitled to such a future, alas, life is not a fairy tale. And false expectations such as these can only lead to spin-sterhood.

Now is the time to outgrow such illusions and start basing your decisions on reality. Cries of "If only he had never been married . . . would devote his life to me alone . . . or could move with me across the planet and never see the X again . . ." will get you zip. You've heard the adage that no one is perfect—though you are damn close—well, he's divorced. That's his imperfection. Accept it. Deal with it. And if he wasn't divorced, he'd surely possess other irksome traits, like an overbearing mother, foul breath, or a craving for glow-up dolls. Pick your poison.

Instead, why not focus on loving him for his idiosyncrasies as well as his assets? Reciprocally, you'd want him to do the same for you. They say that happiness is the ratio between what you expect and what you get. Close the gap and get real.

YOUR ANGER AND RESENTMENT

On the other hand, if you don't express your fears and anxieties upfront, your pent-up emotions will manifest themselves as anger and resentment. A lethal formula for any relationship. Seething thoughts will create an interior dialogue and agenda in your mind that will prevent you from being able to express your thoughts in a loving, nonhostile way. "I hate him . . . how could he do this to me . . . he doesn't appreciate me . . . I'll show him." The rage in your head can become so loud that you won't be able to *truly* listen to your Divorced Man. Be careful, communication breakdown will ensue. Maybe even a psychological breakdown for you. Prozac, anyone? Harboring life's emotional strife can breed physical illness as well. Angry FateMates alone could keep the stomach-relief industry in business.

When talking with your Divorced Man, an angry veneer is self-defeating. You may be saying something that is totally valid, but if you express it with even the slightest hint of hostility, no matter how hard you try to hide it, your Divorced Man will sense it. (And if he doesn't, then why is he so insenitive?) Which do you think he'd prefer: "Darling, we're both so busy, let's schedule some quality time for romance" or "You spend so much time schlepping back and forth, I wouldn't be surprised if you were having an affair with your X"? Though this latter statement may be closer to how you actually feel, which phrasing will get you your desired outcome? If presented irately, your anger will push his hot buttons, his reaction will push your hot buttons, and so goes the brutal cycle that will quickly distance the two of you from each other. If you want a dysfunctional relationship, you might as well move back in with mom and dad.

☞ Reeling & Dealing: One of you will have to see through the irrational behavior born of anger and begin to speak meaningfully from the heart. Guess who? It has been statistically proven that more than 80 percent of the time, it's the woman who brings up difficult-to-discuss issues, while the husband conveniently avoids them. Rise to the challenge.

"But," you may object, "he has so much inner turmoil in his life, the last thing I want to do is add to his misery." Are you actually willing to subjugate your own self-worth so that he can be happy? You martyr, you. Where'd you pick up that impossible complex? Move on, this is the twenty-first century. I'm here to ensure *your* future bliss, what *you* want. We only care about him insofar as he can make *you* happy. If you're not content with yourself first, this can never be a successful relationship.

✎ **TIPS:** COMMUNICATING 101

Between his neuroses (see Chapter 6), and your anxieties (see earlier in this chapter), it's astonishing you can connect with each other at all. But that's precisely what you need to do, particularly when the relationship seems stuck at a certain level of intimacy and you want it to get cozier. The trick is in discovering how to talk through those raw emotions that can either inflame or quell any conversation before you even begin it. Below are fail-safe tips to help you champion the most dreaded conversations.

1. **Prep Yourself:** *Imagine that you are anticipating a romantic evening, filled with sensual pleasures with your Divorced Man. You'd prepare in advance, wouldn't you? Maybe a luxuriant lavender-based bath to calm and cleanse? Or some bubbly, chilled on ice, in your candlelit apartment? How about his favorite perfume strategically dabbed on pleasure-seeking spots all over your body? I could go on and on describing your goddesslike preening; however, in this chapter, that's not what we're talking about. I write this preamble to highlight the need to* prearrange *in order to create the desired* environment *and* mood. *Thinking prior to a potentially heated discussion is an essential part of getting what you want. Consider it your* foreplay *with a Divorced Man.*

Before the conversation, your first goal is to ready yourself so that you are as open and objective as possible. Consider your lessons from *HTMADM:*

- Remove any personal hurt, replays of old nasty patterns, or emotional obstacles you may be experiencing. When you obliterate negative judgments from your mind, you can better empathize, understand, and trust where your

Divorced Man is coming from. You will also be more willing to discuss your feelings of hurt and fear, a necessity for any intense dialogue. If you can think clearly through both your perspective and his, without bias, you can envision more creative integrative solutions to problems that seemed unsolvable only moments before.

- Do not get bogged down in your own feelings of self-pity. Feelings of victimization are born from passivity, causing you to become isolated in your own misery, rather than staying connected to your Divorced Man. Instead, exude confidence, aplomb, and conviction in your quest for deeper intimacy.

- Remember that you're entitled to express yourself. If you don't speak up for yourself, you'll never get what you want. Do not expect him to read your mind (he has enough trouble with his own). Ask for what you believe is reasonable and what you need in the romance. What have you got to lose?

- Submit to the fact that you don't control everything. The pending dialogue with your Divorced Man will be an exchange between two partners. Fifty-Fifty. What he is thinking is just as legitimate as what is racing through your little head. Share, listen, and learn.

- Take responsibility for your actions and choices. You accept the situation and own your decision to be involved with your Divorced Man.

- Formulate a plan. What goal will you achieve during this session? Define it in a statement, for clarity's sake. For example, *My goal is to get my Divorced Man to truly listen to me and not just pay lip service.* Then think through how you two will attain this goal. Have some practical and executable suggestions handy to show him that you've put thought into the matter and to get the ball rolling. Practice having your say beforehand if it'll make the actual conversation flow more fluidly for you.

2. **The Timing and Environment:** *Carefully choose when and where you communicate sensitive topics with your Divorced Man. Just like the anticipated evening of sensuality in the above example, you've got to create the environment that optimizes your desired outcome.*

- Make sure that you've got him in a relaxed and affectionate mental state before you spring any hot issues on him. Not right after work, when he may need time to decompress after a stressful day. Not directly after seeing or speaking with the X or children, when his irrationality level runs high. Not when either one of you is tired, angry, hungry, or within earshot of other people. Not in bed—you'll want to savor this sacred area for eroticism, sleep, and, of course, take-out dinners with video rentals. And preferably not on the telephone, if you can avoid it.

- With your busy FateMate and Divorced Man lives, you may have to coordinate your schedules in advance to designate a time to talk through the hard-to-discuss issues in your relationship. Face it, it's never the right time. What

FateMate in her right mind would rather be having an excruciating tête-a-tête with her Divorced Man than soaking in a fragrant bubble bath with him—actually, this is not a bad place to have your discussion.

If neither one of you is available for a period of time, perhaps you're working late this week to meet a deadline, or he's out of town on business, waiting for the optimal mood and setting for your conversation can mean keeping your emotions bottled up inside for several days—but, don't let it fester beyond one week (there's that ulcer flaring up again!). Suppressing your anger is a wretched existence (for relief, see "TIPS: Anger Busters" on pages 142–145). While you patiently await the inevitable conversation, you're dying to give him a piece of your mind—but don't. Letting your anger get the better of you and catching him off guard will most likely yield unwelcome results that will cause your master plan to backfire on you. Compartmentalize the anger for the time being, staying your sweet FateMate self, until the prescribed time. Your chances for a productive dialogue with successful results that will change his behavior are maximized when you both are open to a loving exchange.

- Limit each discussion session to forty-five minutes. There's only so much of this either one of you can take.

3. **Your Delivery:** *Once you're in the appropriate setting, with a loving mind-set, your next concern is your presentation style. Although I am advising against a FateMate's angry disposition, I am not advocating that you become a dishrag.* Au contraire. *I'm recommending that you consider your presentation style in advance. Be* *honest and think carefully before you speak. It's not manipulative; it's simply smart loving to approach sensitive topics in a warm, inviting, and nonprovoking way. A means to an end.*

- The tone of your voice is equally as important as the words you speak. Begin with a soft, loving, and helpful approach when discussing hard-to-deal-with topics. Otherwise, if you allow your anger to infect your tone, he'll likely feel attacked, criticized, disliked, flooded by your complaints, or judged. Don't trigger these negative sentiments, all of which will set off his defensive buttons and close him off to any integrative advances.

- Take the time first to be soothing. A few extra seconds for a sentence like *"Ever since I fell in love with you one year ago . . ."* will help set the stage, creating the desired effect on him.

- Let loving language pervade your talk. Even though you may not feel it at that moment, call *him "darling," "snoogems,"* or any other pet names that demonstrate affection.

- Physical gestures like holding hands and looking directly into his eyes are meaningful during this time.

- At the right moment, raise issues gently, speaking from the heart about your needs, hurt, and disappointment. Starting your sentences with I rather than *You* is a noncritical way to present your case and will not put him on the defensive. With phrasing such as "I like it when you . . ." or "I feel . . .", you'll be productive in drawing him out of his shell and making him feel that you are a safe place where he can feel free to share. For example, the statement "I'm feeling neglected" is preferable to "You don't care about me." Or, "I would like us to save more" versus "You spend too much money on your children." Be brief and specific when defining the problem.

- Turn your complaints into requests: "You never . . ." becomes "I would appreciate it if . . . ." Again, expressing your anger with civility is important.

- No blaming, accusing, or pouting. When you do so, not only are you pushing him away, but you are placing yourself in the poor-little-me victim's seat, which is antithetical to an empowered FateMate disposition and not where you want to go.

- Say "thank you" liberally. Set the proper example whenever he makes a concerted effort to connect.

- Be prepared to say "I'm sorry" as needed—and then some. Be the first in acknowledging your role in creating and/or maintaining the problem. In general, men have more trouble than women in apologizing, as they perceive it to be a weakness or a defeat. Recognize that these two little words can go a long way with your Divorced Man. Once you get the hang of it, you'll see how easy and rewarding it is to apologize earlier in the argument rather than later.

- While you work at appearing rational to your Divorced Man, which will appeal to his objective side and prevent him from being scared away, allow your emotions to seep into your discourse, but without overdoing it. He needs to feel what you are feeling. Speaking from your heart can be contagious in a way that is most helpful to your discourse.

- As a complement to this, learn when to keep your mouth shut. You needn't express everything that's on your mind. Self-censorship and discretion are powerful things.

- Stay engaged, leading your agenda. Do not withdraw by withholding love, words, information, or sex. It is a passive, if not cowardly, way to control the situation.

- Keep the session a dialogue, not a monologue. Problem solving should be collaborative. Take turns expressing yourselves.

- Resist the temptation to speak in a derogatory manner or sound like a shrink. After reading *HTMADM,* you will be an expert on all the intricacies surrounding your Divorced Man, and may find yourself talking to him as though he were a less-than-precocious two-year-old. The truth is, no one likes a Ms. Know-It-All and it will put him on the defensive, setting you back further.

- When he shares his feelings with you, be receptive and welcome listening to him. Be empathetic, showing that you understand where he is coming from. "I can see how you feel that way . . . ," and so on. Your Divorced Man wants his feelings to be validated and appreciated by you as well.

- Refrain from physically harming your Divorced Man.
When your anger and frustration are more than you can
handle, stop the conversation and politely explain that you
need to blow off steam. (See "TIPS: Anger Busters" on
pages 142–145.)

- Refrain from verbally attacking your Divorced Man. Curtail
any urges to holler, swear, complain, whine, or compare.
It may feel terrific for you, but it'll make him feel like running out the door.

- Never get hysterical. No threatening to jump off window
ledges and the like.

- Cop an upbeat, positive attitude, finding the humor in it
all. Ha, ha!

- Compromise when you're negotiating an issue that
means more to him than it does to you. Two strong per-
sonalities will require meeting somewhere in the middle.

- Pick your battles wisely. Not every irritation is worth fighting over.

- Continually reevaluate your own goals. There's little reason to stay entrenched in a position that is getting you
nowhere.

- If you get uncomfortable with the way things are pro-
gressing, tell him as much and let him know what would
work better for you.

- Exhibit tolerance and patience. That means you'll need to
suspend your urge to sit in judgment of him. This will

enable you to receive his apologies, or attempts thereof.
Give him time to exhibit signs of understanding and development. Always assume that it'll take longer than you'd
like for it to sink in with him.

- Holding grudges may be your natural inclination, but you'll
  have to cut this guy some slack. Try and let the anger slide
  off your back. Your Divorced Man will be making lots of
  mistakes, over and over again, until the fruits of your
  efforts eventually set him right.

- Kiss. Now, move on to that evening of seductive pursuits
  I outlined earlier, if time and desire permit.

Incidentally, it may sound old-fashioned, but there is something to
be said for polite discourse and treating everyone with common
decency. In fact, I would recommend using many of the above tips
in talking to most people you come into contact with, your relatives,
colleagues, greengrocer, etc.

✐ **TIPS:** ANGER BUSTERS

When you feel that overwhelming impulse to flee from his life, or
sense a surplus of venom in your system and acknowledge that the
PC thing to do is to fight the urge to wrap your hands around his
neck, you'll need to reinstill calm in order to put you back in a more
integrative mood. Here are quick fixes you can do prior to your conversation, or even during it, should you need a break to release the
tension. You can do these exercises alone or with your Divorced
Man. Limit any tirades to twenty minutes, maximum.

1. **Listen to music that soothes or transports you.** *No pounding
techno music while racing above speed limits in your car, though.*

2. Call up your best friend and rant away. He or she must be compassionate, objective, and trustworthy so that your anger doesn't
become local gossip, or worse, whispered into your Divorced Man's
or his X's ears. A good buddy with a wise head on his or her shoulders is ideal for keeping things in perspective when you're moving
them out of whack.

3. Smile. It's been scientifically determined that the sheer physical act of lifting the corner muscles of your mouth literally makes
you feel happier. Our bodies are wired such that when we smile,
we produce a mild chemical current that connects with the brain
and makes us feel joyful.

4. Yawn. Releasing the carbon monoxide from your body expels
your toxins and is a proven instantaneous way to relax.

5. Meditate. The following method combines the powers of con-
centration with deep breathing and physical relaxation. As an
accompaniment, aromatherapy is advised.

- Sit in a comfortable chair or lie on your back in a quiet
  setting. Close your eyes.

- Focus on breathing deeply, slowly, steadily. Shallow and
  irregular breaths, and especially hyperventilating, connote
  the storing of stress in the body.

- Make the deliberate decision to clear out all the negative thoughts flooding your mind by concentrating solely
  on an image that relaxes you. Dream of a place where
  you experienced serenity at some point in your life: a
  dense forest, a beach at sunset, a mountaintop, or a
  field of lavender. A sound machine that mirrors nature's

music, such as whistling trees, ocean waves, or rainfall, can be a helpful complement here, setting the right mood and blocking out extraneous noise.

- One at a time, relax your muscle groups. Start with your head and face, paying particular attention to the areas that get most tense, such as the jaw, neck, mouth, shoulders, arms, and back. Then work your way down your body. Tightly squeeze each muscle group, hold for two seconds, then release. Your body parts should be feeling heavier as you continue. Repeat until you've achieved a peaceful state of mind.

6. Exercise. *Go to the gym, take a tae bo class, swing a golf club, speed-walk around the block, or dance (alone is fine, but together is better) till the adrenaline rush from anger has vacated your system.*

7. Get a massage. *Either stroke each other or obtain professional help from knowing palms.*

8. Write things down in a journal. *Remember when you were a young girl and you used to keep a diary? Well, it's time to restart. It's a private, for-your-eyes-only venting facilitator so don't worry about spelling, grammar, or punctuation. Don't be intimidated by the blank page. Start putting pen to paper, free-associate if you like, or doodle away. Write down your fears, dreams, and anything in between. This is a simple and implication-free way to keep track, reflect, and let it all out. Save your musings in a notebook or file, squirreled away from public reach. This will help you forgive, but not forget. In the future, you may opt to refer to your journal to moni-*

tor the progress, or the lack thereof, and even laugh over it with your Divorced Man.

9. Trust. *When you sense anger and suspicions seeping back into your consciousness, make the deliberate decision to trust that your Divorced Man is good and is not purposefully mistreating you. Do this until he gives you reason to believe otherwise.*

LET'S PLAY HARDALL

I know that in the prior section I suggested that withholding love, sex, attention, and a home-cooked meal are cowardly, noncon-frontational, ill-advised routes to take, but sometimes drastic maneuvers are necessary for getting your Divorced Man to comply. In other words, by using *tough love*, and not giving him access to what he wants (you), you drive him mad with desire for that which he can't have (you, again).

Hardball tactics work best when you truly have reached the end of your rope with his postdivorce insane behavior and, for the time being, cannot fathom wanting to see him, sleep with him, or marry him. Now between you and me, of course you still want to see him, sleep with him, and marry him, but you're so damn incensed that your survival instincts kick in and dictate that desperate times require desperate measures.

> *Layla thought she and Bo were well on the road to cou-plehood. They had planned a romantic weekend away to celebrate their recent talks about moving in together. He was to pick her up at eleven A.M. and whisk her off to their favorite getaway in the country-side. Layla had her new lingerie delicately packed in*

tissue and a great bottle of champagne to crack open as soon as they arrived at their hotel.

By eleven-fifteen A.M., Layla was pacing. By eleven-thirty A.M., she was calling Bo on his cell phone, and getting one of those hideous "Out of range" messages. By noon, she was fuming. By one P.M., unpacking. When Bo finally called at two P.M., he explained that he had filled in as a coach for Gus's Little League game—even though it was not his scheduled weekend with his son. Layla slammed down the phone and stormed out of her apartment.

Bo called Layla's apartment repeatedly and each time Layla hung up the phone. Eventually, she just left it off the hook. That would teach him!

☞ Reeling & Dealing: It's best to play hardball after your loving approaches fail and he continues to screw up big time. Use it as a last resort so it remains impactful and he can't accuse you of crying wolf too often or of engineering any disingenuous ploys.

When Layla arrived home several hours later, there were one dozen vibrant yellow roses at her door, and one wilted, wane, apologetic Bo. Layla stepped over the flowers and her "former" boyfriend, ignored his pleas, and slammed the door in his face; but not before informing him that she never wanted to see him again. "Thank goodness we hadn't yet moved in together," she thought. If she had, surely she would have spent the night at Madeline's or checked into a nearby hotel.

> *After a week of cajoling, more flowers, and begging, Bo said the magic words: "I know that I have been acting irrationally where my son is concerned. It's not good for us, and sometimes it isn't doing him any good either. Please give me another chance. I'm more than ready to go into couples' counseling and address my guilt and my propensity to unwittingly harm our relationship, particularly just as we planned a major step forward like moving in together." Quite a mouthful.*

> *It took several dinners, a session with a shrink, and a wonderful weekend away before Layla let Bo back into her life as before.*

Hardball worked for Layla because she wasn't playing a game, or giving an ultimatum she didn't mean. She recognized her own self-worth and knew that Bo's behavior was intolerable. If he thought his actions were acceptable and would go unpunished, well then, he was sorely mistaken. Layla was so infuriated, rightfully so I might add, that she truly never wanted to see Bo again—and he knew it.

Hardball is just as hard on the one throwing the ball as the one receiving it. As the pitcher (yikes, it's that baseball imagery again), you take a risk in his not coming around. And it's excruciatingly painful not seeing or speaking to the one you adore, so make sure that you treat yourself well in the interim. Sip that extra glass of wine, have a facial, go out with friends who make you laugh, or surround yourself in decadence with old lovers who still worship you. Try not to let this temporary purgatory bring you down. Hope that you're one of the fortunate FateMates who can actually be too distraught to eat and shed weight during times of crises.

The best formula: When merited, a cocktail of three parts kindness (as illuminated throughout *HTMADM*) to one part hardball. In
order for hardball to be successful, make sure you really mean what
you say, and can stick to it for the long haul. You may not be able to
get a man to do what you want *when* you want it, but you can get
him to want to do what you want *faster* when you play hardball.

SEEING AN EXPERT

Once you've entered the hardball stage, you know that the problem runs deep; therefore, seeing a worthy shrink is probably the
best investment you can make in a relationship with a Divorced
Man. I cannot say enough about how vital this can be to a couple's
well-being. But I'll try: *See a shrink, see a shrink, see a shrink, see a
shrink.* That's enough for now. Go either solo so you can deal with
your own anxieties that your Divorced Man has so generously
brought to the fore for you, or go together so you can work
through any issues that are hindering your relationship. If you're
lucky, your guy is already in treatment dealing with the post-
traumatic stress his divorce left behind. But don't expect this. Rare is
the man who goes to therapy willingly.

The minute you start getting serious about a Divorced Man,
gather a few names of qualified shrinks. You never know when the
list will come in handy; plus, it's always advisable to select a shrink
when you're not in the throes of despair. The majority of Fate-
Mates begin to visit therapists when they are already in crisis mode,
which is the most difficult time to objectively evaluate a psychological expert. The best references are typically girlfriends you've eye-
witnessed getting their acts together, with Divorced Men in their
lives is always preferable, but even if not. If they recommend their
analysts in glowing terms, these could be considered solid leads.

The best way to figure out the right therapist is similar to a shopping expedition for an ultraexquisite pair of shoes. Look around, try them on, and buy what fits best. By fit, I mean *style* and *comfort*. In terms of style, therapists have a wide variety of approaches. Without boring you with academic explanations of Freudian, Jungian, or other techniques, the net-net here is how interactive are they? Will they be confrontational, telling it like it is, and guiding you in the right direction as they see it? Or will they gently lead you in a more passive way, without much articulation, allowing you to draw your own conclusions? For FateMates like myself who are anxious to cut to the root of their problems, hear an expert opinion, and get results quickly during their fifty-minute sessions, the more interactive method is advisable. Another upside to this is that because it is often faster, it should be cheaper. As for comfort, will you be able to share your innermost thoughts and feelings with her? And does she have an intelligent, inviting, and nonjudgmental manner?

By the way, I use the word *she,* because that's precisely what I mean. If possible, see a female shrink, as she will most likely be more empathetic with your Divorced Man issues than a male shrink. And you need all the support you can get.

✐ **TIPS:** QUESTIONS TO ASK A PROSPECTIVE THERAPIST

*1. **What are your credentials?** These should be prominently displayed in her office. You would probably prefer a licensed and certified social worker or a Ph.D. psychologist, as they have more practical training and experience with one-on-one therapy. Psychiatrists are primarily for when your plight is dire and you are in need of medication. But the truth is that you're already hooked on your Divorced Man, so why compound the problem with a drug dependency if you can avoid it?*

2. How long have you been practicing? *Although longer is not necessarily better, you will want her to be counseling for a minimum of five years.*

3. Do you have experience in working with divorced people? *It's helpful to find a therapist familiar with the issues you are up against. As much as you may feel alone, and that your case is unique, the good news is that you're not and it isn't. Hopefully, your therapist has seen it all before and knows what models work best in such circumstances.*

4. What is your fee and will my insurance cover it? *In this case, obviously less is more, though sometimes you do have to pay up for experience and quality.*

5. How long do you expect my therapy to last? *Depending on how open you are to discussing your challenges—and you should be wide open, with hefty fees like they command, every minute is precious—it may take your therapist several sessions to conclude whether you would benefit best from short-term or long-term therapy. Conversely, it may take you just as long to determine if she is right for you.*

Ultimately, you're seeking someone who is way smarter than you in such matters, professional in her approach, likable so you can establish a meaningful rapport, and at least as old as you are with life experiences to prove it. She should always be trustworthy enough so that you feel comfortable divulging your innermost secrets, but remember, she is not your friend, she is your shrink. That's what you're paying her the big bucks for.

As long as both you and your Divorced Man are secure in your decision to be involved and in your abilities to make it work, your

love can thrive. Check him out. If your Divorced Man is not dedicated to working through the process, then he may not be a long-
term prospect for you. The wonderful news is that it all gets easier
with time. As your relationship advances, you trust each other
more, care more about each other's happiness, and are able to
communicate with more ease.

14. Should I Stay or Should I Go?

By now you've read all about the good, the bad, and the ugly aspects of loving a Divorced Man. It's time to weigh the trade-offs and determine if you want him after all.

BOWING TO YOUR FATEMATENESS

Okay, so you may have self-sabotaging demons in your closet—but who doesn't? Take a deep breath and step back for a moment. You're in love. You've an amazing connection. You're giddy, frisky, and full of hope right now. You think he may be *the one*. You sense that his divorce-related issues might be overwhelming, but you assure yourself that you can handle it. "I'm different than any other FateMate he's ever encountered," you conclude. But can he recognize this? Then again, you wonder whether you're being deluded by the infatuation hormones racing through your body.

Are you the kind of woman to take this risk and withstand all that you may be up against? Will you get what you need out of this? And by the way, what do you expect to get out of this anyway? Love? Sex? Companionship? A family of your own? Financial security? What is *enough* to make you happy?

And what about him? Are his positive attributes worth losing some sanity over when dealing with the mess generated by his divorce? Is he worth it all? Will his X write him a letter of reference? Does he deserve you? Let's find out.

☞ Reeling & Dealing: Ask yourself the following questions to put your future in perspective.

....

✂ **WORKSHEET: IS HE A KEEPER?**

1. How long has he been divorced?

   Up to I year, I–5 years, 5+ years

2. What are the ways in which you are similar to the X?

3. What are the ways in which you are dissimilar to the X?

4. Can you now see the real reasons for why his first marriage failed?   Yes, No

5. What are they?

6. Does he still possess these traits that caused his first marriage to fail?   Yes, No

7. Did he act honorably during, throughout, and after the divorce?

                                                                        Yes, No

8. Is his X antagonistic, potentially posing a problem for you in the future?   Yes, No

9. Does he have any children?   Yes, No

10. What is his relationship to them?   Close, Superficial

11. What is his frequency of involvement?

          Daily, Weekly, Monthly, Vacations, Annually

12. Do you feel this is: Too Little, Just Right, Too Much

13. Are his kids antagonistic, potentially posing a problem for you in the future?   Yes, No

14. Would you want to have a child just like this him?

                                                                        Yes, No

15. Would you want to have a child with him?   Yes, No
16. Do you want to become more like him?   Yes, No
17. Given that his loyalties and resources are split:
    - ☐ Is he loving enough?   Yes, No
    - ☐ Is he rich enough?   Yes, No
    - ☐ Will he want a child with you?   Yes, No
    - ☐ Will he do so within the same
      time frame as your biological clock?   Yes, No
18. Can he separate from his past? (Always assume he hasn't.)
                                                          Yes, No
19. Does he want to and is he capable of evolving as a couple with
    you?   Yes, No
20. If yes, what makes you think so?
21. Has he been self-reflective and/or in therapy since the divorce?
                                                          Yes, No
22. Is he open to couples' therapy with you, if need be?
                                                          Yes, No
23. Would you want to spend the rest of your life with him if he
    never changed from the way he is now?   Yes, No
24. Given all of the above, can you live with this package deal?
                                                          Yes, No

While you ask yourself these pointed questions, you should be reevaluating your relationship, its progress, and the likelihood of its success. Do this every so often, as your answers will change as your relationship evolves. Check your emotional pulse along with the hard facts that your Divorced Man brings to bear to make sure the love is on the right track. Only you can decide if he's worth the effort.

If you're not pleased with your responses, perhaps the timing isn't yet right for the two of you. He might require more developing so that he's farther along his growth curve before you embrace him fully into your life. Take a hiatus until he's ready. Unless he has proved to you that he is capable of and wants to change, don't look for potential. Though we all are born with it, many of us opt not to achieve it. If he shows no signs of advancing in the proper direction—toward you, that is—get going. When FateMates fall in love, we give it our all. Direct your precious love elsewhere; so many others need it.

A friend once wisely summed it up in one thumbnail question: Did he act honorably during his divorce? If the answer is yes, he may well be marriage material. If no, his past behavior may be an indication of his future actions with you.

A Page on Age

You're also concerned that you're not getting any younger. Your age has been creeping up on you and you can't afford to spend one more nanosecond in a relationship that's going nowhere. Then again, you're worried that after this Divorced Man, you may never have another chance at love.

> *Take Madeline. Soon to turn a marriageless and child-less forty, she has reached the frantic now-or-never mode. Madeline's fear—if she pressures Reg with tough love, she might lose him. However, she feels she has no time, much less an inclination, to develop another loving relationship. It could be another two years down the tube. And her tubes aren't getting any younger.*

It's comforting to know that the national average age at first marriage continues to increase. Countrywide, it's twenty-five for women and

twenty-seven for men, while age averages in our nation's major met-
ropolitan areas reach the early to mid-thirties primarily because
these larger populations tend to be more educated and more
career-oriented. And though the usual age difference between a
woman and a man in their first marriage is one to three years, the
age gap widens when a Divorced Man marries a never-been-
married FateMate. Just as we suspected—men do take longer to get
their act together than women. Makes sense since surveys show that
most second wives are in their first marriages.

Recent studies also illustrate that the longer you wait to marry
and the more mature you are in your spousal decision-making process, the better the chances that it will be a partnership for life. After
all, how could a twenty-two-year-old possibly predict what qualities
will be suitable in her partner when she reaches fifty?

☞ Reeling & Dealing: Remember, FateMate, you are a prize. You
acknowledge your self-worth and agree that any man should kiss
the ground you sashay on. This attitude should get his conquistador
juices running wildly. Contrary to what others may tell you, your
age is an advantage. It means you have survived mucho inanities
within singledom and you're all the smarter for it. Only a woman
with your rich experiences can handle a Divorced Man. His issues
are not for the young and the restless.

You've also become an expert comparison shopper, and therefore, you've a clearer idea of what you want in a man and how to
get it. Divorced Men: watch out! A FateMate on a mission always
gets what she wants. And you're not desperate. Although solohood
might not be your first choice, you know you're fully capable of living without a man. Through the years, they've come and gone, but
you still remain your fabulous FateMate self. Keep it up till you meet

Mr. Right. Practice eventually makes perfect. And if you feel he's not a perfect fit after you've applied your *HTMADM* techniques—next! The fantastic news about Divorced Men is that there is always new inventory coming on to the market. With marriage at a 50 percent failure rate, the high turnover means you'll never run out of options. Dating is a numbers game and no one can slow down a FateMate on a crusade.

Unless you value yourself, he won't value you. Research has shown that women who demand a high-quality relationship set high standards as goals. Work at a relationship that has promise, but don't ever settle. I know that you'd rather be single, happy, and independent than miserably married and experiencing the bedlam you've read about in earlier *HTMADM* chapters.

> *After much emotional probing and filling out the* HTMADM *Worksheet "Is He a Keeper?," Madeline judged that Reg was indeed husband-worthy. She felt that he was made for her and that he loved and appreciated her savvy in handling his divorce-related anxieties (if he only knew how heart-wrenching it was to cultivate such savvy!). She also felt better when she consulted her ob-gyn. Her doctor informed Madeline that while her body clock was a-tickin' and bearing children doesn't get any easier as time goes by, that with modern technology, forty is no longer too old to bear children. She was instructed to stop obsessing about her age and talk to Reg openly—just as she would to Layla.*

PART V

MOVING INTO HIS LIFE

❖ 15. Committed! ❖

Hooray! Dreams do come true. You and your Divorced Man are moving in together. The dynamics become all the more intense, but don't let it get tense between you and your Divorced Man.

FateLiving

More than anything, you yearn to create a home that reflects and nurtures the special love you share with your Divorced Man. You envision a warm and inviting abode that makes him feel vital surges of lust serum coursing through his veins, that causes him to lift you in his arms, shower you with succulent kisses, and forget his day-to-day struggles. Good FateMate that you are, you recognize that he's overloaded, so you take matters valiantly into your own hands. And you don't mind. Your take-charge FateMate personality kicks into high gear, hoping to make a swift and seamless transition for him. Nesting instincts you never knew existed consume your waking hours. Fantasies of upgrading the Ikea furniture he hastily purchased years ago when he moved out of his X-home are dancing through your head. (It's no wonder that the nation's high divorce rate has revitalized the home-furnishings and appliance industries.) In the meantime, you're busily mining the dozens of cardboard boxes and files that he never bothered to unpack from that erstwhile time. Continue to save those nasty receipts from his fifth anniversary gift to his X back in 1994? I think not. *Ka-plunk!* Into the garbage where he'll never miss them.

☞ Reeling & Dealing: Although you're anxious to craft your new home into a love den, you'll also have to do the obvious for your Divorced Man, inaugurate your new home life by thinking and acting as a family unit. Alas, your dream home will have to include slight adjustments to accommodate his children. Your Divorced Man, who has the esthetic of a college frat boy living in his dormitory during spring break, only cares about the housing arrangements insofar as it concerns his offspring. Essentially, he wants to provide a homey environment for his kids.

Now, I know as well as you do that the last thing you want is to confer with him on matters of interior design, but go ahead and ask for his input so he sees that you have his children's interests at heart. Even if you ultimately don't take his advice, the overture will earn you brownie points for good conduct.

Therefore, make it easier on yourself by taking his children into account early in the process. Happy cohabiting will take time to adjust to and even more so if you don't adequately provide for his kids. As many FateMates can attest, you'll never hear the end of it from him, or the children, if you don't. With the children's contentment assured, your Divorced Man will be relaxed through what could become a very emotionally strained situation.

The children may feel displaced during the initial transition, so give them time to acclimate to their new environment. If your Divorced Man moves into your existing FateMate home, they may require longer to adapt, as they'll need to be retrofitted into what little space you may have to offer. As a result, they may feel marginalized, versus your relocating to his domicile where they already have a foothold. As the newcomer, though, *you* become the interloper, where your authority can get undermined, not to mention that he won't have enough room to fit your treasured necessities: clothing, objets d'art, toiletries, books, or antique snuff box collection. The best scenario is to move into a new space altogether, where everyone can start afresh, but not all FateMate relationships have this luxury.

The reality is that not everyone has a home large enough to comfortably lodge a FateMate and her Divorced Man's family, not to mention the incorporation of your natural children, if you have any. It's up to you to finesse domestic diplomacy on the big move. Let's count: two adults, possibly three kids, the hovering spirit of the X, two bedrooms, plus one bathroom. And you thought communal living went out with hippies? Home office? That fell by the wayside. Try managing your affairs on the dining room table. Or will that interfere with the children's art projects already spread out on it? You'll have to resort to the haven of your bedroom.

Adjusting your premises will certainly be a tight squeeze, as real estate constraints elicit the darnedest of bedfellows. When visiting, his children can share bedrooms, sleep on bunk beds, fold-away futons, or pull-out couches, if need be. Kids are more resilient than adults give them credit for. And if you position the experience as the next best thing to camping out, they just might buy it. For his kids' toys and peripherals, consider buying a huge chest or trunk so they can quickly make these items disappear from sight. Also, just pray they don't grow, since older children typically connote larger children with larger sizes of clothing and bigger quantities of it, which means they inevitably occupy more space in the home. The upside is that their toys get smaller.

Uh-oh, I hear it already from you FateMates of noncustodial Divorced Men. "But," you insist, "his kids are only there sporadically and I live here full time!" And you're right. Your comfort is paramount and no one would dare to suggest that a FateMate suffer in her own home in any way.

Just remember this simple equation: If the kids are happy, he's happy; and if he's happy, you're happy. So, even though you really need that extra closet space, consider sharing it with his children— I rescind that offer, closet space is too precious, shelf or drawer space will do. Tell them foldable clothes made from synthetic materials are the rage. I know sacrifices like this can be devastating to the fashionista FateMate, but it's a small gesture that will go a long way.

That said, don't be afraid to leave your decorative stamp on your new abode. Go ahead and configure that sexy dream home as you've mostly envisioned it. Above all, don't keep furniture he acquired from his marital home—except if you really love it or it's on the level of a Le Corbusier chair or a signed Picasso lithograph— you both shouldn't have to live with visual cues that remind either of you of his past.

Your Role

The pending "forever after . . . till death do we part" element may put a new spin on how you view your FateMate familial responsibilities. Undeniably, when you live together, everything becomes all the more serious. If all goes as planned, his children will become your children for the rest of your life. Aspiring to this, you are now expected to rev up into high gear the level of your involvement. But all of a sudden the children's sibling rivalry in the backseat of the car on long trips to Grandma's is no longer adorable and becomes downright unnerving. And witnessing how he interacts with the children may now make you cry, "If they were my children, I would never allow them to eat ice cream for breakfast!" We already read that his guilt will motivate him to undergo unparentlike acts such as fueling his kids' sweet-tooth addiction to make sure they return for subsequent fixes, uh, I mean visits. Now and again, you may find yourself longing for the good ol' single days.

Whereas your Divorced Man used to leave you alone while he went to visit his children, now you may consider participating more actively in their lives. Although he should never force you to accompany him on every jaunt with the kids or off-load them on you, certainly you'll be there for important things such as birthday parties, recitals, major sports events, and vacations. But, you also may choose to develop new activities with his children that you can share together without your Divorced Man.

☞ Reeling & Dealing: FateMothering is an acquired taste. Don't fret when it doesn't come naturally; it's not supposed to. Your Divorced Man's children are not yours in the genetic sense, nor will they ever be. In the case of their rearing, although you may be perceived of as in a parenting role, based on your age and relationship with their father, you are actually on the sidelines, with a very limited license to parent and to be perfectly honest, why not be grateful that you haven't this burden to contend with? Unlike other jobs you've mastered, FateMothering is completely *un*institutionalized, without any definition whatsoever. You're operating without any set purpose, road map, or associated tasks; therefore, it's up to you to figure out your role within your Divorced Man's existing family and make it work as best you can.

There is a delicate balance between successful FateMothering and remaining true to your own life. Increasing your time spent with his children amounts to fewer hours with your cherished Divorced Man as well as your favorite FateMate pastimes. This is your balancing act. Discovering the precise recipe for blending ingredients such as joy and obligation is different for every FateMother, so you'll need to determine your own special formula.

As a result, FateMates often feel torn, as if they are living two divergent lives: enticing sexpot girlfriend when his children aren't around; and pseudo-mom, or at the extreme, resentful wench, when the kids are around. Methinks you've the sexpot number down pat. It's the indignant part that requires further elaboration here.

On the one hand, if you sacrifice too much of your hard-earned personal freedom to FateMothering, you may grow to resent his kids, then resent your Divorced Man for introducing this conflict into your life. Subconsciously, you may start picking fights with him on the night before their arrival in anticipation of the dreaded occasion. But in the end, you don't want to resent their presence in your life; rather, you want to enjoy it and grow from it. Besides, the practice can't hurt for if and when you have your own children. On the other hand, if you completely eschew your FateMate duties, you're doing little to strengthen the bond with his children, otherwise known as gatekeepers to his heart, and, therefore, are failing to ingratiate yourself into his life.

✐ TIPS: FATEMOTHERING LESSONS

After canvasing many FateMates, I've compiled a short list of lessons to help you succeed in your new role.

Lesson #1

Do not fall into playing the baby-sitter, maid, chauffeur, butler, tutor, sidekick, buffer between him and his children, disciplinarian, or any other compromising role because you think this will get him to love you more. He should adore you for the dynamic FateMate you already are.

Many FateMates start out assuming these roles, then grow incensed as time goes by. Their once-exciting lives get consumed by his children: picking up after them, making their beds, getting them to soccer practice, etc. FateMates soon learn that household duties are a thankless job anyway. What child would ever appreciate you as a servant? Only a parent bound by blood and DNA coding could possibly derive pleasure from these mundane and beyond-boring tasks. Given your limited free time, it's preferable to contribute in the more enjoyable activities with the kids. Take them to a bumper car rink or playground and see how their faces light up with gratification. Besides, this gives you more quality face time with one another and allows you to have the fun you deserve. Moreover, if you begin as their lackey, your inherited kin will perceive you as such. In effect, you could be conditioning them to be lazy and undervalue your uniqueness, thereby making it difficult for you to return to your former fabulous FateMate self in their eyes, and potentially your Divorced Man's.

Without ever losing your feisty and cool FateMate demeanor, it's within your rights to choose when you take on or forgo Fate-Mothering characteristics. Kindly let your Divorced Man know that you are more than willing to help him out when it is convenient for you and suits your schedule. Meanwhile, he should never forget that they're *his* children, and his responsibility, just as they were before you entered the picture. Besides, there is no reason that a man cannot perform domestic chores just as well as a woman.

Lesson #2

Forfeit controlling every situation, so you don't become the shrew. Ease up and find a livable distance, emotionally, as well as physically, in which to coexist with your new relations. When the going gets tough, if you're caught up in commandeering every situation, it's too easy to fall into a nasty space. So resist all temptation to do so. The last role you want to take on is *you* being the family problem. Let your Divorced Man play the heavy; they'll always love him regardless. Not so with you.

Lesson #3
Set the tone by starting family traditions and responsibilities that are easy and executable. Just like men, children expect you to establish boundaries, so go for it. In this new household, the children are always family members, never guests, and therefore must comply with family rules. Eating meals at the table together, cleaning up their rooms, and making their beds are good beginnings. Other ideas include no television and video games after ten P.M.

Scheduling Quality Times
When the kids' primary residence is with the X, timing becomes particularly problematic. Without confirming the children's visitation schedule, you and your Divorced Man are vulnerable to the X's last-minute whims and crafty machinations. In effect, the X seizes control of your calendar.

> *Once she committed to being a one-man woman, Layla fell head over heels in love with her Divorced Man, Bo. They moved into a new apartment together to mark the start of their new and wonderful future. At this point, Layla decided to step up her participation in Bo's son's life. For a surprise Christmas gift, Layla bought tickets months in advance to the sold-out Ice Capades skating performance. Bo informed the X, but*

*she never confirmed the plan with him. A few days
before the show, the X conveniently decided that a
trip to Aunt Judy's was long overdue, so she told Bo
not to expect them home that evening until nine, the
earliest. At that rate, they wouldn't make it inside the
arena until after nine-thirty, when the show would be
almost over.*

Do you think the X would sabotage the kids' enjoyment in order to
ruin your fun-filled plan? You bet!

☞ Reeling & Dealing: When orchestrating a family event, weekend, or vacation with your Divorced Man's children, advance
scheduling becomes crucial. Your Divorced Man and the X should
schedule visiting days or weekends at least one month in advance, if
possible. This notice should give you ample time to plot out fun
activities with the children.

E-mail is the ideal communication device for planning tasks. It
requires minimum interaction, confirms arrangements, and creates
a paper trail, particularly necessary for absentminded Xs. Take note
as your Palm Pilot becomes your new best friend.

Knowing in advance when you are spending time with the children allows you, in turn, to know when you will *not* be with them,
i.e., you can continue planning for your personal life. Again, without
solidifying arrangements with the X well in advance, you let her
infringe upon *your* own precious free time and that with your
Divorced Man. Translation: less time for loving. Saving and savoring
time for romance is essential to your goal. However, you'll need to
occasionally apply flexibility with the X. After all, you may be the

party requesting a last-minute weekend swap due to an unanticipated business invitation to play golf at Pebble Beach. No one
would ever expect you to pass that up.

Your most essential artillery in these cases is a coterie of
dependable baby-sitters at your disposal so you can enjoy each
other as a couple when the kids are around. For family vacations, if
you enjoy the company of your Divorced Man's mother, invite her
along. The children will have quality time with their grandmother,
she gets a fun trip, and you get more private moments alone with
your man.

◈ 16. Your Children ◈ Together

It's your time to have a child with your Divorced Man. Is this what you call "natural childbirth?"

BABY, MAYBE?

For many, there is no question. Assuming your Divorced Man is able and willing, you're off making babies. Enjoy and skip to the next section. For some of us FateMates who didn't get serious about the mating game until later in life, the baby issue has not been at the top of our agenda—that is, until now. It's caught up with us and we've got decisions to make, quickly. While FateMothering may be rewarding, it has taken its toll. You've begun to wonder if motherhood is all that it's cracked up to be. Furthermore, your Divorced Man may be hemming and hawing about having more children, claiming he's been-there-done-that and from here on in he just wants to lead a life of hedonistic pleasure. After all, isn't that why he's with a funmeister like you? But hey, FateMates want to enjoy their lives too and we love instant gratification as much as anyone else. In fact, having worked hard for most of their adult lives, Fate-Mates are especially ready for a raucous time. On the other hand, we also tend to be goal oriented and serious long-term schemers. We want it all.

☞ Reeling & Dealing: It's wise to have the baby conversation relatively early in the relationship. At first, it doesn't have to be a heavy discussion per se, he just needs to hear where you stand on the matter: pro, con, or undecided which will buy you more time before you declare your position. You'll want to be honest upfront so that you're never accused of baiting him and switching your intent. I've had the dubious privilege of listening to several Divorced Men complain that their FateMates conveniently failed (dare I say blatantly lied?) to introduce the importance of bearing children until later in the relationship, when the men were already hooked. These men felt tricked and harbored a seething anger—that is, until they first held their spanking-new pink baby.

Reciprocally, you need to gauge his disposition. If he has children from his prior marriage, he may be opposed to having kids for a variety of reasons. Financially, the stark reality may be that he simply cannot afford to support two families. He also may no longer want a lifestyle that is encumbered by parental responsibilities. Or, he may feel pangs of guilt that his new baby with you will make him even more guilt ridden (as if that was possible?) over not being there for his children from his first marriage. Then again, he could just feel too darn old to muster up the energy that tots require.

Some FateMates reluctantly forfeit motherhood once they find a discouraging partner in their Divorced Man. If your Divorced Man is against having children with you, he may make it overtly, or even covertly, difficult for you to relish your desire to bear children. For instance, he's conveniently not available for sex just as you're ovulating—how blunt is that?

Another reason you may opt out of parenthood is not having had pleasant FateMothering experiences, or believing you already have your fill of kids in your life. But remember, his children are not your own and, under most circumstances, cannot compare to the way you'll love your own baby. Nature has us biologically rigged as such.

Though having a child at this point may not be his preference, he may agree to have one because he loves you and knows how much it means to you. If he's not enthusiastic about starting a large family for a second time around, maybe only one or a couple of children will do. Or he may be adamantly opposed to raising children at all. Are any of these deal breakers for you? As agonizing as it may be, you will need to thoughtfully weigh the trade-offs to determine if he's Mr. Right after all.

One way to get your Divorced Man to submit to fathering your child is to address his fear of losing you to motherhood. As in many first marriages, his X probably got so absorbed in her offspring that she evaded her wifely duties. This is not uncommon in young mothers who often fail to see the larger picture of maintaining a romance-infused marriage along with the hubbub associated with raising little ones. Fully in love with her children, she gives them all of her passion, at the expense of having none left over for her husband. Your Divorced Man worries that he'll be cast aside again.

But, FateMate, you know better and wouldn't dream of committing the same faux pas. As per *HTMADM*'s advice, part of why he loves you is because you treat him as numero uno. After all, he's been your one and only baby up till now. You've been spoiling him rotten, and so far you've got him where you want him. Now, it's your responsibility to assure him that he's first, today and forever, with or without a baby. Tell him he'll always be your favorite baby and will never have to compete for your attention. Remind him that FateMates are superwomen with lots of love to share.

By the way, deep down, you both know that this is bull. He is well aware, as are you, that, particularly in baby's first years, this defenseless creature cannot possibly fend for itself without its mother's unrelenting care. Reality aside, at least your constant avowals of devotion to him will sound heartening and he'll recognize your intentions as honorable.

And if all else fails, hell, you've been FateMothering his children for long enough—it's payback time. As far as I'm concerned, you deserve to get whatever you want!

ONE BIG HAPPY FAMILY

You may have bargained, begged, or clawed your way in, but once the baby project is green-lighted, there's much to do—allow me to be more precise—there's *everything* to do. If you received even one iota of resistance from your Divorced Man, you can bet that he probably won't be much comfort to you throughout your pregnancy and perhaps beyond. As if incubating a fetus were not already an isolating experience for a new mother, many FateMates complain that they feel like single moms throughout the entire process of pregnancy and thereafter. Not only is he liable to experience the little critter inside you as direct competition for your affection, but he may also perceive it to be a threat to his existing children. Consequently, you may find him to be emotionally and physically absent from this special period of your life as he rushes to spend even more time with his children, which amounts to less time with you since you're busier than ever preparing for your baby's arrival.

And when he does decide to occasionally enter your sphere suddenly he becomes a Mr. Know-It-All. He doesn't want to accompany you to Lamaze classes because it was a waste of time for his first wife (not the least of which is because she delivered by cesarean). So you enroll anyway, and find yourself to be the only one in the class without a mate to support you in your "Breathe, breathe!" exhalations. Well, you can always say he's traveling on business.

The good news is that he doesn't faint at the sight of a dirty diaper and he's an expert at burping a baby.

It frequently comes as a surprise, or more often a shock, to the FateMate system that while you and your Divorced Man were once equals in roles and expectations, after a baby's birth, you immediately fall into old traditional gender roles. Typically, it is the woman whose career gets sidetracked to care for the infant, thereby making her more dependent on the income earned by the man. They say, "You've come a long way, baby," but then why are you ending up like your mother? Or even her mother? And so on. It's as if you struck an implicit deal with your Divorced Man: If the FateMate wants kids that badly, then she will provide the primary care.

While the majority of women with Divorced Men enter the relationship childless, they tend to have babies within the first two years of exchanging their vows. This could very well be a result of the older FateMate age factor here. However, note well, a relevant statistic states that the survival of any marriage is at its greatest risk during the first three years, especially following the birth of the first baby when there is a 70 percent decrease in marital happiness. This is mostly due to the new parents' refocusing on the infant combined with a decrease in energy, sex, sleep, and overall time spent alone as a couple. Interestingly enough, research has shown that in FateMate families, satisfaction rates start low, then climb as you weather the challenges together. This is in contrast to traditional nuclear families where satisfaction rates begin high, then decline as reality sets in.

☞ Reeling & Dealing: Once again, it's up to you to bridge the gap between your Divorced Man's past and present if you want a future with him. My advice? So glad you asked. If you want a child, don't hurry into having one. Why? Because this early period is absolutely the most trying time in any relationship. As you've been reading, with a Divorced Man, there's an extraordinary amount to adjust to and more moving parts than in your typical love affair; a newborn adds complications that many newlyweds cannot endure. Unless your biological clock's tick is deafening, hold off for a minimum of three years after marriage. The longevity of your fulfilling relationship is worth the wait.

That said, he's got to get onboard with the baby notion as early as possible. It's been proven that a man's tenderness during a woman's journey to motherhood fosters a healthier pregnancy. An understanding, nurturing mate can cause a pregnant FateMate to be relaxed throughout what is undeniably a most strenuous time. Your baby has taken over your body; plus, the uncertainty of the unknown, along with the loss of your former identity, are all freaking you out.

Once your bambino enters the world, you'll require more assistance than ever. The experience is often overwhelming, even for the most ambidextrous FateMates, causing you to verge on exhaustion, collapse, and burnout—although, thanks to Marie Osmond, postpartum depression is out of the closet. The natural FateMate tendency is to do everything competently by yourself, but don't dare think you can do this one alone. Cast your super FateMate syndrome aside and enlist your Divorced Man's help immediately. Frankly, that means a minimum of effort on his part: encouraging you in your excitement; emitting positive thoughts about the prospect of a new family; and being available emotionally, spiritually, and physically.

Hoping for parental equality, such as sharing in household duties and familial decisions as they relate to your baby's rearing, is, sadly, unrealistic. This is rarely sighted even in the best of marriages. You may hear him proclaim, "It's your child . . . ," or "I'm doing it for you . . . ," or "Don't expect me to change my life for your kid . . . ," and "I want nothing to do with it. . . ." Calmly explain how alienating this talk is and how couples who love each other think and speak in terms of *us* and *ours,* not *yours* and *mine.*

If he's not actively requesting participation, give him instructions. Don't be shy about composing to-do lists and giving him directives—he may be rusty. Tell him it's a sexy turn-on for you when he assists you with domestic chores and with the newborn. Make good on this statement. With methodical, positive reinforcement from you, he'll soon comprehend that unless he lightens your load, what he thinks he's saving in child care and housework by having you do much of the work is actually costing him romantically and erotically.

Regarding his Mr. Know-It-All streak, if he claims he knows how to change diapers better than you do—good, let him! Be thankful that he's helping out. If he doesn't do it perfectly, don't admonish him or else he'll say, "Fine, you do it then!" And if he doesn't help out, but still persists in being a backseat baby swaddler, he'll have to ease up on you because you will want to learn for yourself without his dictation.

✐ TIPS: BRINGING HOME BABY

Introducing your extended family to one another is not always a picture-perfect Kodak moment. Your Divorced Man will want all the kids to get along and play together like one big happy family, but chances are that there may be an age gap between his first and second sets of children; therefore, they may have little in common with one another. The great news is that you have built-in baby-sitters.

To minimize any potential conflicts when bringing your new baby into your existing Divorced Man's family, take the following advice:

1. As you start trying to get pregnant, have your Divorced Man casually mention to his children that the two of you are considering giving them a baby brother or sister.

2. Once you've conceived and decide it's time to safely announce to the world you are pregnant, let the kids be one of the first to know.

3. Immediately start referring to them as the baby's sisters and brothers, not half-siblings.

4. As the delivery time nears, give them each a creative baby-related task to do in preparation for the birth: constructing a family tree, or designing a wall hanging to place above the baby's crib.

5. Let them call a relative with the news of the baby's delivery.

6. Include photos of his children in the baby's book.

7. If they are old enough, let them hold the baby and care for it for short periods of time.

8. Tell them the baby loves them.

9. Keep them apprised of the baby's development when they are not around: E-mail photos, etc.

10. If possible, spend time alone with your Divorced Man's children, away from the baby.

So what did Madeline finally do? She heeded HTMADM's advice. Once she got over her morbid fear of being alone at forty, she made the conscious decision to speak to Reg openly about her anxieties, all the while not putting too much pressure on him. On the three-year anniversary of his divorce, they celebrated, at first passionately, and then on another evening with his two teenage daughters. Madeline got back to relishing the love and companionship she had established with Reg before she got into the mommy mode.

And guess what? She got pregnant! It was as much of a surprise to her as it was to Reg, a very thrilling and welcome surprise for the two of them. Even Iona and Adele were delighted by the prospect of an infant sibling who would elevate their seniority in the family.

There was a lovely June wedding at Madeline's parents' home with just a hint of belly showing in her designer wedding ensemble, supplied wholesale, of course, by Layla, who stood weeping beside her as a bridesmaid, while Reg and Bo looked on expectantly.

And now united, Madeline and Reg have a treasured new baby boy and they are living ecstatically ever after.

◈ 17. Getting the Last Word In ◈

The decision is yours to make.

Remember, the ultimate goal is twofold: to get him to love you *and* to see if he is worthy of your love. *If* you want this relationship, it's yours for the taking. Its success is largely based on how much you want it after reading *HTMADM*. Just as in accomplishing any hard-won objective, it will require some degree of tenacity, risk, compromise, and much internal growth on your part. Making intelligent FateMate choices will get you what you want, it just may take longer than you want it to. Similar to the way you handle your finances or your career aims, if you want this man, stay the course. Think long term. Stay in control. FateMates have their work cut out for them all right, but the rewards of love are deep and plentiful. The more *HTMADM* time and energy you put in initially, the bigger and better he'll return his love. In the end, sharing your life with the man you love is what *HTMADM* is all about.

And finally, with marriage and a child together, you can drop the *Fate* prefix and refer to yourself as a *Wife* and a *Mother.* Your Divorced Man then becomes your *Man.* You have established a family unit all your own.

Acknowledgments

A most special thank you to Paula Namer, C.S.W., psychotherapist. This book could not have been written without your expert insights, professional and creative contributions, and infinite enthusiasm. I am forever grateful.

And of course, much genuflecting and appreciation to the dynamic women (some FateMates themselves), who made it all possible: Judith Regan at ReganBooks/HarperCollins, my publisher and chief visionary; and Christie Fletcher at Carlisle & Company, my agent and champion. Lastly, kudos to Brian Saliba at ReganBooks, my editorial white knight.